Additional praise for *Searching for Alpha* . . .

"*Searching for Alpha* successfully combines fascinating anecdotes with a unique and valuable insight into modern investing. I highly recommend this book!"

—Frank Jones
Executive Vice President and
Chief Invesment Officer
The Guardian Life Insurance Company
of America

"A random walk through the investment minefield with practical applications in laymen's terms. *Searching for Alpha* is an essential read for all investors who want to learn how to improve their portfolio returns."

—Brian Cornell
Managing Director
Mesirow Advanced Strategies

"*Searching for Alpha* is a great book! It will help many investors understand why their portfolios can occasionally produce disappointing returns, even though the market's current direction and sentiment is positive. More importantly, it spells out some steps that they can take to maximize their chances of investment success. But perhaps its most important contribution is to make everyone aware that when it comes to markets, there are no magic bullets."

—Greg Newton
President, MAR Hedge

"In this period of unprecedented valuations, *Searching for Alpha* brings us down to earth with invaluable guidance on the risks and returns of investing. All investors can profit from this book."

—Paul Merriman
President, Merriman Capital Management

SEARCHING

for

ALPHA

Other books in the *Wiley Investment* series

SEARCHING

—— *for* ——

ALPHA

The Quest for Exceptional
Investment Performance

Ben Warwick

John Wiley & Sons, Inc.
New York • Chichester • Weinheim • Brisbane • Singapore • Toronto

Published by John Wiley & Sons, Inc.
Published simultaneously in Canada.

This publication is designed to provide accurate and authoritative information in regard to the subject matter covered. It is sold with the understanding that the publisher is not engaged in rendering professional services. If professional advice or other expert assistance is required, the services of a competent professional person should be sought.

AIMR^{SM} is a service mark of the Association for Investment Management and Research (AIMR). John Wiley & Sons is not affiliated with AIMR.

Library of Congress Cataloging-in-Publication Data:

Warwick, Ben.
    Searching for alpha : the quest for exceptional investment performance / Ben Warwick.
        p. cm. — (The Wiley investment series)
    Includes bibliographical references and index.
    ISBN 0-471-34822-8 (alk. paper)
    1. Investments. 2. Stock exchanges. 3. Securities. 4. Mutual funds. 5. Portfolio management. I. Title. II. Series.

HG4551.W37 2000
332.6—dc21   99-059987

To my mother,
and the memory of my father

Foreword

In the 1930s, the stock market was considered by the average investor as questionable in reputation, polluted with stories of insider trading, manipulation, abusive brokerage commissions, and in many circles, a replacement for the local gambling establishment. But then came individuals like Sherman Adams, the creator of the first open-ended mutual fund (the Massachusetts Investors Trust), who had the foresight and understanding of properly organizing stock investing; who believed that the stock market could evolve into an investment medium that was well respected by the most conservative investor. An investment that forged all barriers from the average household to the largest institutions in the world. A market that could change the supposition of fiscal and monetary economic policies, becoming the very fabric of our economy by providing the main source of capital infusion into thriving companies throughout the world.

As my career has unfolded over the past 20 years, I have seen the alternative investment world provide a similar evolution to modern finance. I have seen alternative investments redefine the understanding of traditional risk management, portfolio analysis, and investment techniques of individual investors, corporations, and institutions. These markets have changed the way corporate officers manage the risk of their business, as well as the employment of new, noncorrelated investment instruments that greatly enhance traditional stock and bond holdings. The academic world has been presented with investment instruments that have pushed modern portfolio theory into new areas of discovery: new ideas that dispute the classification of an asset class, sophisticated strategies that have taken advantage of historic pricing models, and the motivation behind a multitude of studies on the traditional thinking of beta and alpha analysis. The alternative investment world has evolved from an investment medium unrecognized by the majority of traditional financial and academic establishments to a flourishing industry that has garnered attention from some of the brightest minds of our time.

These minds have been the catalyst behind the accumulation of a library of academic studies that have challenged and expanded the thinking on traditional investments, while documenting the value and substance of alternative investments. Such names as Harry M. Markowitz, William Sharpe, and Merton Miller come to mind. Other factors that have contributed to these studies over the past 20 years include such milestones as the availability of the personal computer in the late 1970s and in more recent years the exponential growth of on-line technology and information. All of this has provided the computing power for the practical employment and advancement of pivotal financial models. Some of these monumental advancements include the creation of such paradigms as the capital asset pricing model and arbitrage pricing theory.

Within the initial chapters of this book, an important foundation is laid on the world of indexing. This entire concept is a by-product of the efficient market hypothesis that continues to spawn a debate over passive versus active management. A debate that encompasses the evaluation of inherent returns, the random nature of markets versus the efficiency or lack thereof in various marketplaces, and the quantification of beta and alpha. This debate is mainly embraced by the academic and institutional worlds, although the substantial growth of several prominent index mutual funds over the past decade is evidence that participation has occurred from a fragment of individual investors. Stock index funds had their genesis in the early 1970s and presently capture approximately 30 percent of the assets invested in this area. Indexing of alternative investments is truly in the rudimentary stage while the industry is busy defining its unique aspects. Yet, I would expect the indexing of alternative investments to have consequences similar to those encountered by traditional indexed product.

Overall, this book attempts to present the history and usage of traditional stocks and bonds, as well as alternative investments. It has taken a hard and candid look at these investment fields, asked some brusque questions that are not always popular with your neighborhood broker, and attempted to give you honest and factual conclusions. It is intended to give some intuitive insight into the investment world that is not openly published. Many of the stories are based on fascinating, unique events in history, with the intention of providing a parallel concept to key financial benchmarks that have changed and shaped our investment world. Mixed within these stories are key quantitative and qualitative models that are intended to require you to stop and evaluate past thinking while considering the fundamental truths of finance. Finally, this book introduces several creative business ideas that are intended to help you evaluate your current investment practices.

I hope you are equally entertained and educated as you search for value that can be added to your investment portfolio—alpha.

RICHARD BORNHOFT

Preface

We all know how cruel the truth often is, and we wonder
whether delusion is more consoling.

Henri Poincare (1854–1912)

Horatio Alger, Jr., was the author of more than one hundred books that
inspired young people from the post-Civil War period through the end of
the nineteenth century. The heroes of his books always had the same
qualities—morality, courage, generosity, and perseverance. Alger's tales
held that everyone, no matter how poor or powerless, could overcome
any obstacle and achieve their dreams. More than 250 million copies of
his stories have been sold worldwide.

If Mr. Alger were alive today, he would no doubt be puzzled by the
investment management business. Few would deny that investment professionals are intelligent, hard-working individuals who operate their
businesses in a morally upright manner. But how could so many well-
meaning people get it so wrong? In 1998, for example, only 17 percent of
all stock mutual funds beat the unmanaged basket of stocks that comprise
the Standard & Poor's (S&P) 500 index. Over the past five years, only

one of the largest 45 stock funds beat the S&P 500 index—and by less than one percent per year. Can anyone win the investment game? That question is the focus of this book.

Part One details the advent of modern portfolio theory and its off-spring, the capital asset pricing model. These theories form the basis for today's investment industry, which invests trillions of dollars in the world's stock and bond markets. We also examine the evolution of index funds, a powerful concept that has changed the way both individuals and corporations invest their money. Actively managed mutual funds—those controlled by investment advisors who utilize various strategies in an attempt to beat the market—are also an important focus of the book. Investors should be aware that the inability of these funds to generate consistent, superior returns are largely due to one factor—both the managers and the mutual fund companies are simply not motivated to do so.

Part Two introduces some investment styles that may be used in concert with a traditional portfolio of securities (stocks and bonds) to produce exceptional performance. Arbitrage, which seeks to exploit pricing inefficiencies in a variety of markets, is a compelling strategy that can produce handsome profits, but not without attendant risks. Arbitrage pricing theory, another extension of modern portfolio theory, attempts to classify market risk into its most elemental forms and is the foundation for a number of strategies in the equity and fixed income markets. Finally, the use of derivatives—among the most misunderstood of all financial instruments—is considered.

Part Three of *Searching for Alpha* begins with an examination of that inevitable antagonist, taxes. As we shall see, taxes are often the largest impediment to the creation of efficient portfolios, yet less than a handful of published studies have examined their effects on the investing process. We also consider a fascinating new field—behavioral finance—and discuss how its theories can help explain the existence of market anomalies. The impact of technology on the investment management industry is also examined.

Along the way, you will be introduced to a fictional cast of characters and their struggle to appropriately invest their client's assets. Many of the questions posed by these characters represent some of the most untenable problems faced by investors today. Unfortunately, these dilemmas can be neither described fully nor unraveled completely in this book. But as professionals who constantly operate with uncertainty, volatility, and incomplete information, we must embrace the critical issues that challenge our mettle. Problems are never solved by ignoring them.

BEN WARWICK

Denver, Colorado
April 2000

Acknowledgments

I want to thank those who made a work of this magnitude possible. Special thanks must be given to Adam Whitehead and Richard Bornhoft, two persons without whom this book would have never been possible. I would also like to thank Brian Cornell, Albert Hallac, Chip Hayes, Don Plotsky, Chad Leavitt, Eric Roseman, Edward Fishman, Will Sorrell, Lane Carrick, Joe Hannan, and the members of The Bornhoft Group team— Ron Montano, Bob McMorris, Nancy McMorris, Russ Nuzum, Bernard Wilkinson, and Nancy Hamilton—for their consideration during the process of writing this book.

B. W.

Contents

PART TWO: FREE LUNCH, ANYONE?

Arbitrage trading has produced attractive returns with negligible volatility. This popular strategy and the true risks of participation are examined.

Arbitrage pricing theory, which attempts to categorize market risk into a small number of components, is contrasted with the capital asset pricing model, which states that the return of a stock is directly related to its risk relative to the overall market

As the asset class with the bad reputation, derivatives are blamed for everything from the stock market crash of 1987 to excessive speculative activity in the capital markets. Meanwhile, proponents of futures commonly utilize these flexible instruments to construct portfolios that need minimal funding and that protect portfolios in times of extreme volatility. The history—and the promising future—of the managed futures industry.

Market neutral programs allow investors to participate in strategies that are not correlated to the movements of traditional investments like stocks and bonds. But what happens when asset classes move in unison? A postmortem examination of the market meltdown of August 1998.

PART THREE: THE BUSINESS OF ADDING VALUE

PART ONE

PERCEPTION
AND REALITY

Searching for Alpha

Chapter 1

The Equation That Changed the Investment World

The term *alpha* (α) refers to that portion of an investor's return that is due to the skills of an investment manager, rather than the returns of the overall market.

Harry Markowitz got it right the first time. As a young University of Chicago student searching for an appropriate doctoral dissertation, a professor suggested that he investigate the stock market. In the late 1940s, this was an unusual subject for serious academic study. The memories of the Great Depression, along with the well-publicized scandals of such market luminaries as Richard Whitney (the Chairman of the New York Stock Exchange who was caught in a stock fraud scheme with his brother) and J. P. Morgan (recently vilified by a congressional subcommittee on banking and finance) generally soured the public's view of stocks as a viable investment medium. Many people believed that it was possible to make money in the stock market only if one were an insider or possessed inside information.[1] In addition, the proliferation of so-called bucket shops—brokerage houses of ill repute that charged outlandish commissions and manipulated stock prices—only served to further separate the stock market from the average investor. Encouraged by Marshall Ketchum, then dean of the Graduate School of Business and coeditor of the *Journal of Finance*, Markowitz was directed to *The Theory of Investment Value*, at the time the definitive book on the subject.[2] Authored in 1937 by John Burr Williams, a stockbroker turned Harvard graduate student, the book

3

instructed its readers to construct a concentrated portfolio of stocks that trade at prices below their intrinsic value. According to Williams

> Wise investment requires that only such issues as are selling far below their true worth should be bought; then, as large income payments are received in subsequent years because things turn out better for the security than most people expected, a handsome return on the principal can be enjoyed.[3]

There are significant differences between an investment in a single company's stock versus that of the market as a whole. The former involves selecting a stock that trades at a low price based on its earnings potential, current dividend rate, or future prospects. The latter is better described as a long-term investment that grows with the nation's fortunes. But the prospect that the bulk of an investor's return should emanate more from one's ability as a stock picker rather than the direction of the overall stock market was the prevailing thought at the time. For a pragmatic man like Markowitz, this concept seemed horrifically out of place. In his words, as he read Williams's tome in the library, "I was struck by the notion that one should be concerned with risk as well as return."[4] This fortuitous thought was to become the foundation for a revolution in investment management. His theories also allowed a way to quantify that portion of return that results from skill, and not just the direction of the market. This value-added component of an investor's total return would eventually become known as *alpha* (α).

Markowitz's views about the stock market led to the publication of a paper titled "Portfolio Selection" in the March 1952 issue of the *Journal of Finance*. What made the paper so innovative was its emphasis on constructing the proper *portfolio* of securities rather than merely picking what seems to be the best individual stock. Markowitz's views were based on his belief that investors should have little in common with gamblers who are willing to risk their entire net worth on one investment, and more in common with rational decision makers who prefer to spread their risk among various asset classes like stocks, bonds, and real estate. In this example, the rational investor would prefer to maximize his expected *utility*—his return in relation to his risk tolerance—rather than maximizing his return with no regard for the risks involved (Figure 1.1). Such efficient portfolios would give owners the most bang for their buck—the highest return for a given level of risk.

The idea that investors will avoid risks for which they are not compensated is the focal point of Markowitz's study. And there is much evidence to support the existence of such rational behavior. First, people buy insurance, and they pay large amounts for the privilege, well beyond the actuarial value of the losses. Second, it turns out that risk aversion follows necessarily from another cornerstone of economics—that people are willing to take risks to achieve wealth, but once wealth is achieved their risk tolerance decreases. This principle was introduced by Oscar Morganstern, an economist, and John von Neumann, a mathematician, in their book *The Theory of Games and Economic Behavior* (1944).[5]

But this is not to say that people are at times irrational. "I can calculate the motions of the heavenly bodies," Sir Isaac Newton wrote, "but not the madness of people." Newton had an IQ of 190, yet neither his intellect nor his scientific thinking could prevent him from losing £13,000 in

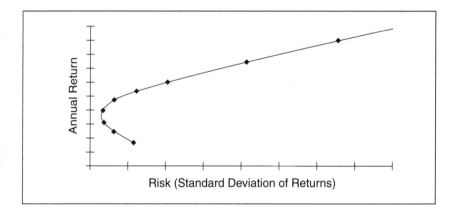

Figure 1.1   Markowitz's Efficient Frontier (1952)
Markowitz's efficient frontier (1952). The part of the curve extending from point A and above designates the optimum return for a given amount of risk. This scientific method of investing was in stark contrast to the more speculative activities at the time of Markowitz's discovery.

the South Sea Bubble.[6] The South Sea Company was formed in 1711 by a group of English merchants, who paid off the British national debt of £10 million in return for a 6 percent interest rate and exclusive trade rights with South America. Although the company never profited from their monopoly (and, indeed, failed to transact any business whatsoever), the prospects of such a scheme were so tempting that people fell over themselves for the opportunity to participate. By 1720, the expectation of immense profits drove the company's stock up 1,000 percent in just a few months. The ensuing collapse of the stock's price nearly brought down the English government.[7]

History points to periods when the psychology of the crowd overwhelms the rationality of men, reducing them to lemmings who follow each other off a craggy cliff to a certain death. Nowhere is this more apparent than in the world of investing. And since Markowitz's theories depend on the sagaciousness of market participants, a number of well-respected professionals took exception to his conclusions.

One of the more notable examples was Gerald Loeb. A successful stockbroker and author of the best-selling book *The Battle for Investment Survival*, Loeb was typical of the successful operators of the day. Opposed to buying and holding a diversified portfolio, Loeb preferred to put all of his eggs in one basket—and watch the basket. A value investor to the core, he preferred out of favor issues to have the highest potential reward. "The great fortunes," Loeb said, "are made by concentration."[8]

Loeb was no doubt influenced by John Maynard Keynes. In his 1936 book *The General Theory of Employment, Interest, and Money*, Keynes reasoned that professional investors should focus their energies on analyzing how the crowd will value a security "three months or a year hence."[9] Keynes, in other words, applied psychological principles rather than financial evaluation to the study of the stock market. He saw the market as a beauty contest, where the only thing that mattered was the opinion of the judges. In this instance, it was much more sensible to choose the contestant that the judges will pick, rather than one's personal favorite. Likewise, an investment should be selected based on what someone else is willing to pay. In Keynes's mind, it was perfectly logical to pay three times what something is worth—as long as there is another investor willing to pay even more. This approach has been commonly referred to as the greater fool theory.[10]

On the subject of diversification, Keynes said "a small gamble in a large number of different companies where I have no information to reach a good judgment, as compared with a substantial stake in a company where one's information is adequate, strikes me as a travesty of investment policy."[11] Keynes's method of investing earned him several million pounds for this account, and a 10-fold increase in the market value of the endowment of his college, Kings College, Oxford. *The General Theory* sold nearly five million copies. Keynes's philosophy would, nearly 60 years later, seed a new theory of investment—behavioral finance—that is the topic of Chapter 10.

A growing volume of research reveals that people yield to inconsistencies, myopia, and other forms of distortion throughout the process of decision making. But the lack of rationality was not the primary reason the most successful investors of the time shunned diversification. Indeed, the investor in the early 1950s faced several obstacles in constructing an efficient portfolio. The first was transaction costs. At that time, commissions costs were fixed by the Securities and Exchange Commission (SEC) and averaged about 2 percent per transaction (i.e., $200 to buy or sell $10,000 worth of stock). Constructing a well-diversified portfolio would have been quite expensive during this period—transaction costs alone would have consumed a considerable amount of the return of the stock market (commissions today run about 90 percent less than these levels).

Further, there were few bargains to be had in the mutual fund industry. In 1950, mutual fund companies had only two billion dollars in assets at the time, which in this day would equate to an average-sized stock fund. The front-end loads charged by these funds (the markup tacked on by the selling agent as compensation) averaged 8–10 percent. Thus, there was only one way investment managers could hope to beat the high expenses incurred by their clients—by actively managing assets, in the hope that a few well-picked stocks would skyrocket in price. The investment managers during this time had huge bogeys to overcome, and the only way to offer decent returns to their investors was to attempt to beat the market.

And then there was the math problem. In order to utilize Markowitz's approach, two separate calculations were necessary. First, the expected return of the security had to be determined. Second, one had to estimate the covariance (or relationship) for every stock and bond being considered. Although such calculations are now routinely done on PCs, in 1961 the best commercially available IBM computer required more than 30 minutes to analyze a 100-security portfolio.[12]

Still, Markowitz had set the stage for a revolution in the realm of investment management. His most powerful concept—that return is inextricably linked to the risk one is willing to take—proved to be both intuitively simple and computationally mind-boggling. It would take the contribution of three more academicians, all of whom eventually won the Nobel Prize in their respective fields, to bring the revolution to light.

$$\alpha$$

To the professional money manager, Markowitz's efficient frontier presented a curious paradox. As a fiduciary, an investment advisor is charged with the responsibility of structuring an investment mix that best matches the risk and return parameters of their clients. Thus, a risk-adverse retiree would have different objectives than a young professional saving for retirement.

Therein lies the paradox. The efficient frontier defines the portfolio with the best possible reward-risk characteristics. Can a fiduciary justify the use of tailor-made (and suboptimal) portfolios, simply because clients have differing risk aversions? And how can one best vary the results of the portfolio—on the basis of both risk and return—to conform to the client's best interest?

The answer to this question had its origins in a most unlikely place. Prior to the Great Depression, most economists believed that economies functioned according to Say's law, which states that the very act of producing goods generates an amount of income exactly equal to the value of the goods produced (i.e., supply creates its own demand). This concept was also applied to the labor market. One of the tenets of the so-called classical school of economics was that the economy was capable of providing for the full employment of the economy's resources. It was acknowledged that now and then abnormal circumstances would arise in such forms as wars, political upheavals, droughts, speculative crises, and so forth, to push the economy from full employment. But it was contended that when these deviations occurred, automatic adjustments within the price system would soon restore the economy to the full-employment level of output. The classical economists came to embrace capitalism as a self-regulating economy where full employment was regarded as the norm. Thus, in an economy capable of achieving both full production and full employment, government intervention could only be a detriment to its efficient operation.[13]

One embarrassing fact dogged the classical school of economics: prolonged periods of unemployment and inflation. Whereas the classical approach might explain a minor recession, a severe market dislocation such as the Great Depression was difficult to dismiss. Thus, a significant area of interest to economists in the 1930s was to find a better, more realistic explanation of the forces that determine the level of employment.

The publication of John Maynard Keynes's *The General Theory of Employment, Interest, and Money* was at the epicenter of this effort. Described by John Kenneth Galbraith as "a work of profound obscurity, badly written and prematurely published," *The General Theory* nonetheless successfully attacked the classical economists' contention that recession would cure itself. His basic policy recommendation—a stark contrast to the laissez faire approach of the classical school—was for government to increase its spending in order to induce more production and put the unemployed back to work.[14] Indeed, the massive unemployment of the worldwide depression of the 1930s seemed to provide sufficient empirical evidence that Keynes was right.

It is not difficult to understand the popularity of Keynes. Not only was he one of the most influential economists of the twentieth century, he was also a principal representative of the Treasury at the World War I Paris Peace Conference; a deputy for the Chancellor of the Exchequer; and a leading figure in the Bloomsbury Group, an avant-garde collection of intellectual luminaries who greatly influenced the artistic and literary standards of England. He also made time to run an investment firm and organize a ballet company.[15] But it was the speculative side of Keynes's nature that led to his theories on the level of interest rates. One of his underlying assumptions was that each investor would choose between cash and risky assets based on his or her expectations on interest rate changes. He reasoned that investors who expected interest rates to rise would want to hold all their capital in cash, while those who expected rates to fall would want to hold risky securities (stocks and bonds) that would benefit from such a scenario. He never considered a situation where an investor would consider a combination of the two. Likewise, Markowitz assumed that investors would select securities from a menu consisting solely of risky assets. Thus, the only risk-reducing technique in the Markowitz universe was diversification.

This idea intrigued James Tobin, a distinguished economist at Yale and a leading proponent of the Keynesian approach. Tobin reasoned that investors do not limit themselves to either-or decisions. Rather, rational individuals combine risky assets with cash to arrive at an acceptable limit of risk. Thus, regardless of the investment objectives of the individual, the optimum portfolio of securities—the one that offers the best risk-adjusted return as defined by Markowitz—is always the correct asset mix for all clients. If one is interested in a lower return with less risk, a cash component should be introduced to the mix; for more aggressive investors, one could borrow money (on margin) to increase exposure to risky assets.

This concept came to be known as Tobin's theory of separation.[16] It greatly simplifies the task of choosing the best portfolio for a given situation, because it is always the portfolio that offers the best return/risk ratio, regardless of the investor's objectives. In fact, when Tobin explained his work during an impromptu press conference in 1981 (shortly after the announcement that he had won the Nobel Prize), he simply said that the theory dealt with diversification—"don't put all of your eggs in one basket." Shortly thereafter, Tobin was sent an editorial cartoon that showed the Nobel Prize awarded to a doctor explaining how his award was for "an apple a day keeps the doctor away."[17]

α

Although Tobin's contribution was a significant step in the development of modern portfolio theory, the laborious calculations required to determine the efficient frontier were still quite formidable. No one was more aware of this than Markowitz. In 1960, he invited William Sharpe, a UCLA Ph.D. student, to develop a way to make the problem more tenable. Sharpe completed a paper on his ideas, which was published in the January 1963 issue of *Management Science*.[18] He reasoned that the variation between stocks had many causes, but is most dependent on one underlying risk factor. This factor, above all others, determines the volatility of a stock's price.

The factor turned out to be the stock market itself. About one-third of the variability of a stock is due to the movements of the stock market as a whole. The balance is due to a bevy of influences particular to that stock, such as a strike, an overly positive or negative earnings announcement, or company fundamentals. Sharpe called the stock's variability due to general movements of the equity market the stock's *systematic risk*; the remainder was termed the stock's *unsystematic risk*.

Sharpe's idea for separating risk into two distinct categories introduced several very interesting properties. First of all, Sharpe said that systematic risk cannot be eliminated by diversification. Because stock prices move more or less in tandem, even a well-diversified portfolio will exhibit wide variations in price. Systematic risk is the risk of being in the market, and it cannot be avoided unless stocks are not part of a portfolio.

The numerical descriptor of systematic risk was eventually referred to by the Greek symbol beta (β). Beta is essentially a comparison between the movements of an individual stock (or portfolio) and the movements of the market as a whole. The calculation begins by assigning a beta of 1.0 to a broad market index, such as the Standard & Poor's (S&P) 500. If a stock has a beta of 2.0, then on average it swings twice as far as the market. If the market goes up 10 percent, the stock should rise about 20 percent. If a stock has a beta of 0.5, it tends to be more stable than the market (the stock will go up or down 5 percent when the market goes up or down 10 percent).[19] Thus, the relationship between the returns of any two stocks can be related simply to their difference in beta.

If the beta concept were accepted universally by all market participants, then how would the stock market behave? If this were the case, low beta (i.e., low risk) stocks would be more highly valued than riskier stocks with higher betas. Portfolio owners would, therefore, be willing to pay a premium per share for the low beta stocks, which would cause their expected return to decrease. Meanwhile, the share prices for the high beta stocks would have to decrease enough to create demand for buyers. The high beta stock prices would have to be low enough to provide a *risk premium*—a higher return—to entice investors to hold them.

And this is exactly the type of market equilibrium that has been observed. Common sense dictates that investors must be compensated for taking additional risk. Hence, less risky stocks have lower expected returns than more risky stocks.

Unsystematic risk is another matter. Because unsystematic risk can be eliminated by adequate diversification, Sharpe reasoned that it is a risk that need not be taken. Thus, since it can easily be avoided, he insisted that *unsystematic risk has little or no bearing on the value of a stock.* In other words, investors demand higher returns for stocks with risks that *cannot* be diversified away—stocks that move up and down in sympathy with the portfolio—but they do not expect to earn a premium for stocks with risks that *can* be diversified away.[20]

Sharpe presented his ideas in a 1964 *Journal of Finance* article titled "Capital Asset Prices: A Theory of Market Equilibrium under Conditions of Risk."[21] The concepts he expounded became known as the capital asset pricing model, or CAPM (Figure 1.2). Eugene Fama of the University of Chicago Graduate School of Business coined the term "one factor model" to describe Sharpe's notion of beta as the "most important single influence" in determining a stock's value.

Other papers have confirmed the CAPM. But some studies have found that the actual risk–return relationship is much flatter than predicted by the CAPM. In other words, low-beta stocks earn higher returns, and high-beta stocks earn lower returns, than the theory predicts.[22] This is a phenomenon much like that found at the race track, where long shots seem to go off at much lower odds than their true probability of winning would indicate, whereas favorites go off at higher odds than is consistent with their winning percentages.[23]

Many studies have concluded that the CAPM is not valid, either in the short run or the long run, in explaining returns from securities. This is to be expected. Like all capital market theories, CAPM makes a number

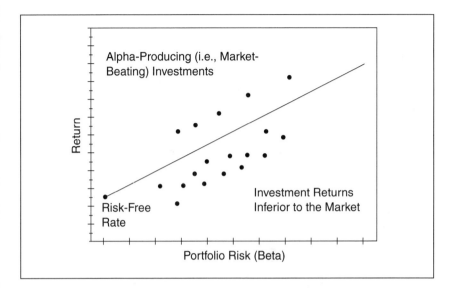

Figure 1.2   **Beta and Returns**

According to the capital asset pricing model (CAPM), the return of an investment is directly related to its beta (β), which is a comparison of the investment's volatility relative to the market as a whole. Investment managers who can generate returns in excess of the market return (or alpha) appear as dots above the line.

of simplifying assumptions that do not hold up in the real world. In fact, CAPM assumes no transaction costs, no taxes, limitless short sales, and no constraints on lending or borrowing. But even in its simple form, the CAPM captures many strands of investment theory and market behavior remarkably well. Its theoretical significance is equaled if not surpassed by its widespread use in business and finance.

But what about the supposed holes in the theory? If the CAPM were true, everyone would own the same portfolio (individuals with differing risk aversions would utilize more leverage to increase their return). And because unsystematic risk would have no bearing on a stock's value, security analysis would add no value. The somewhat irregular fit of the CAPM to the real world leaves an open door, albeit a narrow one, to innovative portfolio managers who just might uncover a large enough wrinkle in the theory to consistently beat the market. Part Two examines just how narrow this door is.

α

There is perhaps no other battlefield where victory is so lavishly rewarded as Wall Street. Performance is so revered that the New York Stock Exchange was built to resemble an Egyptian temple replete with animistic symbolism. Investment pros intent on finding an edge have developed varied methodologies, including technical analysis, fundamental analysis, Elliot wave theory, astrology, and even chaos theory to determine the mood of the markets. An anecdotal glance at an issue of the *Wall Street Journal* would seem to indicate that most have been successful, as evidenced by the number of advertisements touting the "best performing mutual funds" over the most convenient time frames (1 year, 3 years, 5 years, or since inception).

A significant outgrowth of the CAPM has been the development of a number of models that quantify investment performance. Although the models differ from one another, all of them attempt to reduce the two dimensions of investment performance—risk and return—into a single measure.

Performance indicators were first used to measure the savvy of mutual fund managers. There were three reasons for this emphasis. First, mutual fund returns have always been readily accessible, since by SEC mandate their track records must be made available for existing and potential investors. Second, mutual funds have attracted enormous assets in the last 20 years; they account for the bulk of the $7 trillion invested on behalf of individuals and pension plans. Lastly, with such a potentially large audience, funds compete vigorously for new clientele. With so many funds clamoring for new investors, claims of superior investment performance had become a mainstay in fund advertising. Performance measurement was needed to separate the wheat from the chaff.

To best quantify the value added from active investment management, the return of a mutual fund is commonly divided into two components. The first component is the return of the market in which the fund is active. For instance, for a stock fund that invests solely in high-capitalization issues, this first component would be the return of a broad market index measure like the S&P 500. Thus, if a manager took a passive approach (i.e., bought all of the components of an index), the fund would garner the returns of that index, less management fees, sales fees, and commissions. The second component of a mutual fund's return is the amount of additional return an investment manager can generate from actively buying and selling. Thus, if the S&P 500 index rose 12 percent in a year, and the fund gained 14 percent, the added value of active management would be +2 percent. This added value is referred to as the Greek symbol alpha (α), which was originally defined in the CAPM. Of course, one must account for risk in the generation of increased returns. If our fund manager gained 2 percent over an index, but his monthly returns were twice as volatile as the underlying index, his alpha did not come from his market acumen—he simply relied on strategies that were much riskier than a simple buy-and-hold approach. In a bear market environment, this manager will most likely expose his clients to far more risk on the downside than a passive index investment. Thus, our definition for alpha is two pronged. An investment manager is said to generate alpha under the following circumstances:

- Alpha is generated if investment returns exceed an appropriate benchmark, if the risk taken to achieve the return is similar to that of the benchmark.
- Alpha is generated if managers' returns are equivalent to an appropriate benchmark, if the risk taken to achieve the return is less than that of the benchmark.

Before the work of Markowitz and Sharpe, evaluating the performance of an investment advisor was difficult simply because there did not exist a universally accepted method for doing so. By using the terms *beta* (a measure of market risk) and *alpha* (a measure of excess return), both of which trace their origins to the CAPM, the skill level of professional investment managers can easily be compared.

But in order for the generation of alpha to occur, mispricings or other anomalies must exist for investment managers to exploit. The efficiency of the capital markets, and its effects on manager profitability, is the focus of Chapter 2.

Chapter 2

The Revolution of
Indexed-Based Investing

> I can't believe that the great mass of investors are going to be
> satisfied with just receiving average returns. The name of the
> game is to be the best.
>
> *Edward C. Johnson III*
> *Chairman, Fidelity Advisors*

The next big question that needed to be answered was a matter of degree—to what degree is the market predictable? There are two sides to this
issue. The first side, maintained by legions of active portfolio managers,
claims that thorough analysis allows them to beat the market—either on
an absolute basis (by achieving a higher return than the overall market) or
by achieving comparable returns to the market with far less risk. These
managers sell more than just the possibility of market-beating performance. They give us hope that the intellectual achievements of humans can
overcome the virtually perfect efficiency of capital markets. Their message
is clear—that technology and intuition are powerful allies in any venture
and can surely produce results superior to those obtained by pure chance.
Judging by the percentage of assets under advisement by active managers
(about 70 percent of total invested funds), it appears that the message has
been well received by both professional and individual investors.

The other side of the issue is the somewhat sober viewpoint that the
markets are so devilishly efficient that it is improbable that any traditional manager can match its returns over a long period of time. The first

evidence to support this view emanated from aspiring French mathematician Louis Bachelier, in his 1900 doctoral thesis, "The Theory of Speculation." Bachelier, using a rigorous scientific approach that became the groundwork for the theory of probability, found that fluctuations in stock prices were largely random in nature. Unfazed by this brilliant piece of scholarly research, the great Jules-Henri Poincaré, Bachelier's faculty advisor, found the thesis "somewhat remote from those our other candidates are in the habit of treating."[1] Bachelier never managed to get a job in mathematics, and his thesis was ignored for nearly half a century. The response to Bachelier's work was typical for his time, as the collaborations that followed between the art of investment and the science of math and statistics were largely ignored.

All of that changed in 1965, when Nobel Laureate Paul Samuelson published, "Proof that Properly Anticipated Prices Fluctuate Randomly," a paper that used techniques similar to Bachelier's to highlight the high degree of randomness in day-to-day stock prices.[2] As a brilliant piece of work by a well-known and respected researcher, Samuelson ushered in a new era of market study. University of Chicago professor Eugene Fama furthered the effort when he defined the term *efficient market hypothesis* (or EMH) in 1970, by stating that "at any given time, asset prices fully reflect all available information."[3]

There are two broad categorizations to the efficient market hypothesis. The *weak form* of the EMH states that past prices are useless in determining future prices. Such an idea is supported by a number of studies that have shown no correlation between what happens today and what was observed yesterday.[4] Those who ascribe to weak-form inefficiencies belong to one of two groups. One group, the chartists, study price history in the belief that they can identify price patterns that give an indication about future behavior. A second group follows the momentum of stocks, with the belief that if information is incorporated slowly into security prices, a sudden move in either direction can give an indication of the market's future direction. Both groups use only price information (or, in some cases, changes in trading volume) to make their decisions, shunning the more accepted fundamental factors, such as earnings per share and book value. The so-called school of technical analysis maintains a large and loyal following on Wall Street.

The *strong form* of the EMH asserts that all public information is fully reflected in asset prices. If this view of the EMH is a valid description of the markets, then securities selection based on fundamental information—earnings growth, dividend yield, and other popular indicators—should yield no more profit than randomly throwing darts at a list of stocks. In fact, many studies have shown that fundamental information is as difficult to predict as the stock market itself. A 1962 study presented at a seminar for financial analysts showed that growth in earnings per share in one period was only 6 percent correlated with growth in the prior period; 94 percent of the change in earnings growth were random fluctuations. The study concluded that projecting future earnings growth from historical earnings is a useless exercise.[5] As one would expect, the strong version of the EMH has stirred much controversy since it was proposed. Its implications are profound—that fundamental analysis is doomed, that what hundreds of investment analysts do for a living is fodder, and that the $100 billion investment industry that manages trillions of dollars provides no real value.

At first glance, the evidence to support the theory that markets conform to both the weak and the strong form of the EMH is exceedingly voluminous. On closer inspection, the case becomes even more compelling. After adjusting for risks taken, few (if any) investment managers systematically produce returns above that which could have been achieved by chance. Furthermore, performance figures on institutional investors do not seem to be predictive of future success. The entire process of selecting an investment manager based upon past performance seems hollow. But when the theory first challenged institutional investors in the mid-1960s, their response was to ignore the possibility of efficient markets. Academics simply did not enjoy high regard in the investment arena. After all, in the 25-year bull market to 1966, many people had made vast sums in the equity markets. Why should one listen to a teacher who obviously had not made the same fortune?[6]

The academic community considered itself to be the sole underpaid advocate to the efficiency of the stock market. The investment practitioner, essentially institutional in nature, considered the academic as a challenger. The rift was caused partly by the fantasy that investment advisors were omniscient. They believed that if the alchemy they performed to turn conventional wisdom into profit were understood, they would all be unemployed. Thus, investment managers surrounded themselves with elaborate and expensive testimonials which, although related to good results in the past, seemed to gradually lose their potency. Just as the drought questions the value of the priest's rain dance, so does a bear market humble the professional stock picker.[7]

To determine how effectively actively managed portfolios fare, it is necessary to have a benchmark available to use as a comparative tool. It should come as no surprise that the academic community was one of the first advocates for such a tool. One of the most notable calls for a benchmark came in 1974, when Paul Samuelson insisted that "some large foundation set up an in-house portfolio that tracks the Standard & Poor's (S&P) 500 index—if only for the purpose of setting up a naïve model against which their in-house gunslingers can measure their prowess."[8] One year later, investment consultant Charles Ellis, the author of the well-respected book *Investment Policy*, noted that 85 percent of institutional investors had underperformed the return of the S&P 500 index. Ellis cited the main culprit as fees: if equities return 9 percent per year, and annual fees totaled 2 percent, active management must return 11 percent on a gross basis just to equal the return of the index. His conclusion was simple: "If you can't beat the market, you should certainly consider joining it. An index fund is one way."[9]

The ideas for the first index fund went back a few years earlier. In 1969–1971, Wells Fargo Bank had worked from academic models to develop the principles and techniques that led to index investing. John A. McQuown, William L. Fouse, and James Vertin pioneered the effort, which culminated in the construction of a $6 million index account for the pension fund of Samsonite Corporation. The scheme was to hold an equal dollar amount of each of the 1,500 stocks listed on the New York Stock Exchange, which seemed the most appropriate proxy for the stock market. But the execution of the idea turned out to be a "nightmare." Some stocks moved more widely than others, and a few moved in an opposite direction from the pack, so that the equal weighting would not stand still. Heavy transaction costs were incurred from the constant reweighting back to the original equal dollar amounts.[10]

Sensing that it was on to something big, the bank remained undaunted at this first attempt at indexing. To avoid the perils of investing in an equally weighted index, Wells instead focused its energies on a market-weighted portfolio. Since a market-weighted index adjusts to rising share prices, one must only buy all the stocks in an index when the account begins. Adjustments are only required when stocks are added to or removed from the index, which lowered transaction costs. In 1973, Wells Fargo set up a commingled fund available for eligible trust accounts that would track the performance of the market-weighted S&P 500 Composite Stock Price Index. The Wells Fargo effort has been a model for all of the index funds that followed.

α

Three problems remained before index funds enjoyed widespread acceptance by investors. The first problem, and the most cumbersome, had more to do with the law than with the stock market. The Employee Retirement Income Security Act of 1974, or ERISA, requires that an investment be "prudent," and extends the liability for any imprudent investments to corporate administrators and board members who oversee pension plans. Trust law holds that in considering whether an investment is prudent, one must look at every stock in a portfolio, not just the portfolio as a whole. Thus, investments designed to duplicate a market index, while ignoring the merits of the particular stocks that make up the index, could be ruled imprudent under ERISA.

By early 1976, The U.S. Department of Labor still had not issued an opinion on index funds, but it did issue a policy statement that prudence questions involving mutual funds would be decided on the basis of diversification, not on the basis of particular stocks. Meanwhile, the index funds then in existence handled the issue by screening out stocks of troubled companies—not for investment reasons, but because their lawyers insisted on it.[11]

And then there was a problem with commissions. Until the mid-1970s, commissions on the buying and selling of stock were fixed by the New York Stock Exchange. Although the actual cost varied with the size of the order and the price of the issue, a typical commission bill came to about 2 percent of the value of the transaction. Even though index funds involved negligible buying and selling, transaction costs did occur when new investors added money to the fund, existing investors redeemed shares (stock liquidation was needed to raise cash), or stocks were added to, or deleted from, the index. Fixed commissions resulted in an average *tracking error* (the shortfall between the fund's return and the return of the index) of about 1 percent in the early 1970s. One percent sounds reasonable in a bull market, but in the 10-year period ending in 1975, the S&P 500 index increased at an annual rate of only 3.5 percent. Thus, trading costs consumed nearly one-third of the return of the index!

The era of fixed commissions ended on May 1, 1975—a day tearfully referred to as "May Day" by brokerage firms. In this newly competitive environment, transaction costs tumbled; a trade that might cost 70 cents a share to execute could be done for as little as 5 cents a share. A bright new day dawned for index investors.

The final problem to be solved was more philosophical than operational. Investors who defer to an index fund shun all other stocks not represented in the index. In effect, any company that is not in the S&P 500 index (by far the most widely replicated index) will never be purchased by indexers unless an existing S&P 500 stock drops out of the rankings so that another stock is included. And if the stock market is efficient because of the efforts of equity analysts in identifying undervalued stocks, these issues would not be purchased by pension funds if all of their assets were committed to an index strategy of large capitalization equities like the S&P 500. Thus goes the argument, the stock market would not be as efficient if index strategies ruled the roost.

Indeed, the increased institutionalization of investment management has proved to be troubling for smaller firms. One common criticism of institutional investors is that they created a two-tier market. But it is not clear that the growing popularity of indexation has compounded the problem. Few large investors at the time were willing to hold stocks in companies that were not in the S&P 500, mainly because of ERISA's prudent man clause. More importantly, it is debatable whether it is the business of pension funds to keep the markets efficient. Presumably, their only concern should be to maximize the returns of their constituents and to forget about the efficiency of the stock market until it appears that there are enough "inefficiencies" to profit from them.[12]

Finally, are markets efficient because of the efforts of analysts in finding attractive issues for their clients? Undoubtedly, one of the main reasons that markets respond so quickly to new information is that there is such a large number of intelligent, capable analysts following the vast flow of available information. But there does not seem to be a shortage of buyers for undervalued stocks. Many of the 6,000 or so mutual funds available today (there are more funds than listed stocks) specialize in these types of issues. Thus, the evidence is less than conclusive that the increased popularity of indexing by large market participants would decrease the efficiency of small-cap stocks.

α

Within this environment the first index fund available for individual investors began operations. The chairman of the Vanguard Group, John Bogle, says that the idea first presented itself to him during the completion of his 1951 senior thesis at Princeton University. He concluded that to maximize the future growth of the mutual fund industry, a reduction of sales loads and management fees would be necessary. He also had the foresight to suggest that funds should avoid "making claims for superiority over the market averages."[13]

Designed to track the movements of the S&P 500, the First Index Investment Trust (now called the Vanguard 500 Index Fund) began trading on September 1, 1976, with $11 million in assets. True to his previous research, the fund had a management fee of 0.20 percent—one-tenth of the standard 2 percent fee charged by other funds at the time. Vanguard had originally hoped to invest in all of the stocks in the S&P 500 index in their exact proportions. But due to the small size of the fund, only 280 stocks could be purchased—the 200 largest stocks (which represented almost 80 percent of the weight of the index), plus 80 stocks selected by various optimization models to match the profile of the index.[14] As fate would have it, the fund was launched at the exact worst time. The S&P index experienced a five-year slump where it was outpaced by the majority of its actively managed counterparts. But the boom in the stock market that began in 1982 took "Bogle's folly," a name euphemistically given to the Vanguard 500 Index Fund, along for the ride. At the end of 1997, the assets of the fund had grown to nearly $70 billion, ranking it the world's second largest equity fund. Meanwhile, of the 45 largest stock funds (all those with more than $2 billion in assets), only one has beaten the S&P 500 index over the past five years—and by a scant 0.60 percent per year (Figure 2.1).[15]

Even as indexed assets have soared to over 30 percent of all pension assets, its most vocal supporters are claiming that the growth of the strategy has been a disappointment. William Fouse, dubbed the "father of indexing" for his pioneering work at Wells Fargo, looks at total assets in such funds as a percentage of market capitalization and wonders why the idea hasn't gained even more favor. "Twenty-five or so years ago," he commented in 1991, "I would have forecast that index assets by now should be on their way to 75 percent or more of institutional equity assets."[16] Reflecting on it all, Fouse suggests that while he won the battle, he lost the war. The "traditional establishment has won, hands down, with strong assistance from the pension consulting community." Many consultants, he added, "haven't been pragmatic with regard to the practical aspects of index management. Lots of consultants accommodate indexing, but don't really like it."[17]

But not all hold the same pessimistic point of view. Richard Ennis, a well-known pension consultant, estimates that indexing will soon reach 50 percent of the institutional market. But both he and Fouse agree on one important issue—that fees generated from indexing will continue to decline dramatically. "From a business perspective," Fouse says, "I am convinced that index fund managers are intent on self-destruction."[18] What was originally a business with a 0.20 percent annual fee is now, he says, headed even lower. Fouse recalled that his firm (Mellon Capital Management) recently lost a very large portfolio to a competitor for a "zero

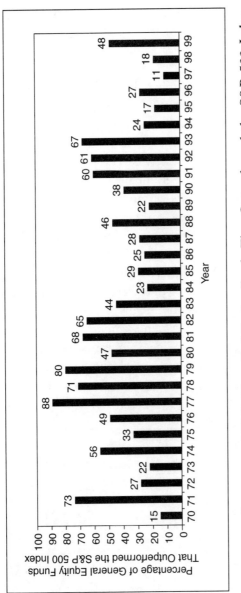

Figure 2.1 Percentage of U.S. Diversified Equity Funds That Outperformed the S&P 500 Index, 1970–1999

The returns of actively managed mutual funds have consistently lagged behind the performance of the overall market. The biggest contributors to this trend are investment management fees and transaction costs.

Source: Based on data from Lipper Inc.

percent fee." Not only are firms using indexing as a loss leader, which in-creases their assets under management, it also gives them a chance to enter the high-margin business of stock lending (where stock is loaned to short-sellers for a fee). With such low fees, the number of new entrants in the indexing business will be sharply reduced. The likely result is that in-dexing will be a highly concentrated business, with a handful of firms each managing close to $1 trillion in assets (Figure 2.2).[19]

If indexing is poised for further growth, assets are destined to decrease in some sectors. Assets will most likely be lost in two areas. As one might expect, the biggest area is actively managed large capitalization U.S. stocks (i.e., managers who operate within the S&P 500 index). The huge armies of analysts who cover these stocks make the sector tenaciously ef-ficient. It is doubtful that any large-cap manager has the skills to consis-tently beat the S&P 500 index. Active management in this sector will continue to be, in the words of Fouse, a "loser's game."[20]

Indexing is even more alluring in the taxable bond market. Managers who specialize in fixed income are usually benchmarked to the Lehman Brothers Aggregate Bond Index, which is composed of 66 percent in U.S. government securities and 34 percent in investment-grade corporate bonds. This index, which has an average weighted maturity of about nine years, returned approximately 8.50 percent per year during the 1990s.

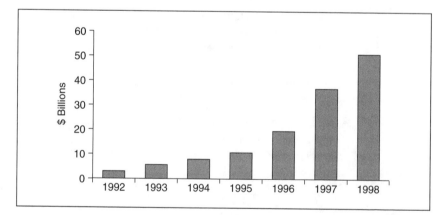

Figure 2.2   Total Net Cash Flows into S&P 500 Index Funds ($ Billions)

Considering that the average actively managed bond fund charges about 1.10 percent per year, it comes as no surprise that few managers can beat this benchmark. If one were to divide a group of bond funds into fifths based on annual expenses, one would find that the bond funds with the highest expenses had the worst performance.[21] This fact seems to be lost among mutual fund managers; over the past five years, expense loads for taxable bond funds have increased 14 percent.[22] There will likely be a move to bond index funds that will rival that in equities.

Better prospects for active managers exist abroad. One area is the global bond markets, where the lack of a well-accepted benchmark has prevented firms from developing a passive methodology. Similar arguments can be made for U.S. small stocks. According to Morningstar, the mutual fund ratings service, nearly one-half of all small stock funds beat the small-cap Russell 2000 index in the five-year period ending in 1999. These areas do not have the wide analyst coverage of large-cap U.S. stocks, so tradable inefficiencies may still exist.

$$\alpha$$

Investors should consider index funds as an efficient way to get the diversification they need without the added expense inherent in actively managed funds. But the index revolution has not solved all of the problems inherent in the investing process. What started as a low-cost way to invest has instead turned into something of a monster. In their never-ending quest for more client assets, mutual fund companies have started creating their own indices and designing funds around them. There are now index funds based on Internet stocks, raw materials prices, and the stock markets of such countries as Malaysia and Austria. Some of the 265 index funds currently in existence boast huge expenses and generate substantial capital gains taxes for their unfortunate clients. It is probably a bit naïve to consider the current indexation movement as an opportunity for mutual funds to create a sensible, low-cost product. A better understanding of the mutual fund as a business entity should shed some light on the objectives of the firms that operate and profit from them.

And that is the focus of Chapter 3.

Chapter 3

Can Anyone
Outperform the Market?

> If people are disappointed with their mutual fund returns, it
> may be because their expectations are too high.
>
> *John L. Steffens*
> *Vice Chairman, Merrill Lynch*

As we have seen, the historic stock market appreciation experienced in the latter half of the 1990s has not been kind to actively managed mutual funds. Since 1994, there has not been a single year where more than 25 percent of actively managed funds beat the Standard & Poor's (S&P) 500 index. In an effort to maintain the popularity of active management, investment advisors have begun touting their returns during periods of declining stock prices. These advisors note that in years when equities produce negative returns, holders of actively managed funds have experienced periods when their investments have beaten the returns of their respective indices. In essence, active managers who promote this philosophy regard their higher fees as an insurance policy against market declines. "Sure, those index funds look good as long as the market keeps going up," these active managers tell their investors, "but we'll come through when the market starts dropping. You'll need an expert hand to guide you through those dangerous waters," they caution.

The perfect year in which to evaluate the promise of active management to produce attractive returns during periods of declining stock prices and increased market volatility is 1998. Instead of the broad market advances that made indexed funds the investment of choice in the last decade, in 1998 a select handful of stocks performed spectacularly enough to take the market indices to new highs. In fact, 14 companies accounted for 99 percent of the S&P 500 index's returns for the first three-quarters of the year. Moreover, just a handful of stocks made up the gains in the S&P in the fourth quarter of 1998, and two stocks alone—high fliers Microsoft and Dell Computer—produced one-third of the gains. By year's end, the S&P 500 index returned 28.5 percent, and the NASDAQ fared even better—up 40.1 percent. In short, 1998 was a year for stockpickers—an environment where a portfolio consisting of a selected few issues would have trounced the returns of the overall market. So how did the active managers fare?

Unfortunately for the throngs of individuals invested in such funds, 1998 will be remembered as one of the worst years for actively managed mutual funds in history. Out of the approximately 1,500 domestic equity funds, one-third of them trailed the S&P 500 index by 10 percentage points or more—and one-third of them actually lost money (less than 50 percent of the remaining one-third beat the index). The recent carnage was far more severe than the industry experienced in 1990, when the S&P 500 index lost 3.12 percent (the average fund lost 5.90 percent), and in 1994, when the index was essentially flat (and nearly one-third of funds beat the S&P).[1] To understand the baffling results of active management in 1998—and, for that matter, the paltry performance of mutual funds in general over the last 20 years—it is important to consider how these funds work and what their objectives are.

α

Like basketball, the mutual funds are a uniquely American institution. The fund industry can trace its roots to a shrewd military contractor for George Washington's army, Daniel Parker. When Washington's army was released from duty in 1783, some of its members had not been paid for up to two years. Parker agreed to help the newly formed government meet its obligations, but he demanded that the soldier's payments would take the form of notes redeemable for goods purchased in his chain of mercantile stores.

Parker realized that the American soldiers were so desperate for cash, they were willing to sell their notes for any amount. And as a close associate to Alexander Hamilton, Parker also knew that the government would eventually allow the notes to be converted to hard currency at face value. So when the notes dropped to five cents on the dollar, Parker pooled funds from a group of wealthy European financiers and bought as many of the notes as he could find. Eight years later, the certificates were trading near one hundred cents on the dollar. The incredible success of this, the world's first mutual fund, allowed Parker to live out his years a wealthy man, ensconced in a palatial French chateau.[2]

The period after the Civil War witnessed a reemergence of mutual funds. With the growth of the American economy in the late nineteenth and early twentieth centuries, many types of financial institutions appeared in the United States to provide a means for the growing prosperity of the country to be invested. But as the bull market of the early 1920s propelled such popular issues as Nash Motors ($110 per share) and Boston Insurance Company ($683 per share) into the stratosphere, it became increasingly difficult for an individual investor to own a diversified portfolio of stocks. In 1924, stockbroker Sherman Adams decided to pool the shares of such companies into a mutually owned fund, in which investors could buy or sell shares at net asset value. He attracted a total of $50,000 from two hundred investors, and the result was the first open-ended mutual fund (i.e., the fund continuously offered new shares and redeemed existing shares daily). The Massachusetts Investors Trust is still in existence and currently manages about $12 billion in customer assets.

During the period prior to the Great Depression, mutual funds were largely unregulated. Funds commonly used leverage to enhance returns and did not have to disclose their fees and expenses to their customers. In the aftermath of the 1929 stock market crash, the U.S. Congress directed the Securities and Exchange Commission (SEC) to study investment companies and make recommendations for reform. This culminated in the passage of the Investment Company Act of 1940 (the 1940 Act), and the Investment Advisers Act of 1940 (the Advisers Act). These acts required adequate disclosure with respect to investment companies and prohibited self-dealing between investment companies and their affiliates.

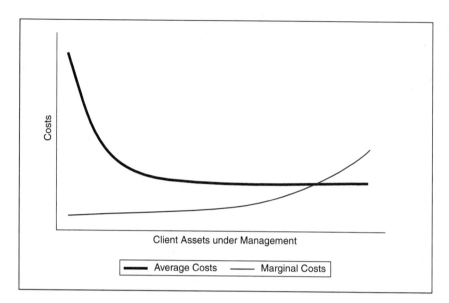

Figure 3.1   **Average and Marginal Costs**

As client assets grow, the incremental costs associated with managing additional dollars decreases. This phenomenon is referred to as an economy of scale. Mutual funds reach their optimum level of fee generation when average costs equal marginal costs. At this point, any additional client assets raised will incur additional costs to the fund operator.

But even with these widespread reforms, from 1940 through 1980 mutual fund sales grew at a paltry rate of about 5 percent per year. This did not sit well with fund operators, who knew that increased assets meant a disproportional increase in profitability. This was due to the industry's *economies of scale* (Figure 3.1). Simply put, scale economies exist when extra output (in the case of funds, the management of additional customer dollars) does not result in a concomitant increase in expenses. Put another way, for an established fund, increases in customer assets allow for higher and higher profit margins, until funds reach a point where costs associated with running the fund exceed additional revenue. But during this period of slow growth, few mutual funds could reach this level of maximum efficiency (Figure 3.2).

Desperate for more client assets, the mutual fund industry began to lobby Washington for permission to pass advertising costs to fund investors. This arrangement, argued the industry, would have two benefits

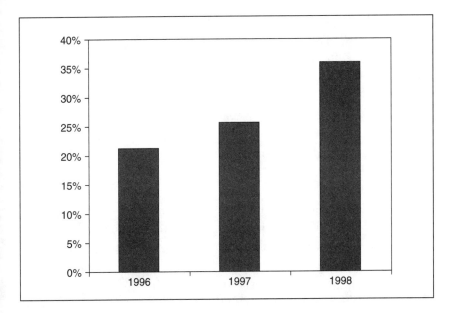

Figure 3.2   **Profit Margins for Mutual Fund Companies 1996–1998**
Source: Based on data from Robert Morris Associates' *Annual Statement Studies.*

for the economy. First, the increase in advertising would likely increase assets in mutual funds, which would allow mutual fund companies to pass economies of scale to their clients in the form of lower overall costs. Increased advertising would also encourage Americans to invest more money, which could further strengthen the U.S. economy.

The result of this effort was the passage of rule 12b-1 by the Securities and Exchange Commission, which allowed mutual fund companies to pass the cost of marketing, distribution, and advertising expenses to the funds' existing shareholders. As expected, mutual fund executives quickly discovered that the use of these so-called 12b-1 fees (which range from 0.20 to 1.0 percent per year) had a dramatic effect on industry profits, which transformed mutual fund companies from stodgy institutions to marketing powerhouses.

As much as SEC rule 12b-1 has been a windfall for the mutual fund industry, it has remained a bust for fund investors, as the promises made by industry executives to lower fees have never come to fruition. In fact, since 1980 expenses paid by shareholders have actually *increased* more than 30 percent. Through this rule, mutual fund companies had found a way to transfer the costs of marketing to their customer base, which not only reduced fund returns but also increased industry profits.

Besides increased marketing, larger mutual funds companies use another strategy to increase assets—acquisition. Most studies have found that mutual fund companies achieve full economies of scale when client assets reach $20 billion to $40 billion. Failure to achieve such an asset base has caused some small-size fund complexes to be absorbed by more cost-efficient fund groups that can offer the same products at lower costs.[3] The investment management business has seen rapid consolidation (Figure 3.3), with about 20 fund families per year being purchased by a larger rival. After a merger, funds with similar objectives are often combined, which has the effect of burying the performance record of the weaker fund, because

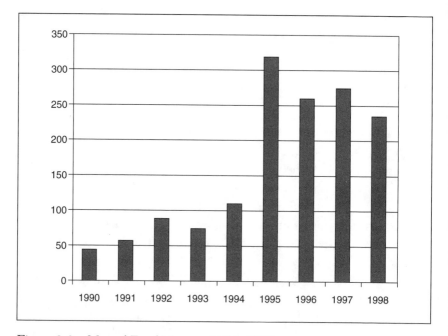

Figure 3.3   **Mutual Fund Mergers 1990–1998**

Source: The New York Times, August 16, 1998, p. BU 11. Reprinted with permisson, NYT Graphics.

the surviving fund generally assumes whichever track record is better (as well as the name of the better-performing fund, if possible).

α

One of the most profound ways that mutual fund companies have adjusted to the astonishing growth in client assets is by an increasing dependence on trading technology. The era of electronic trading began in 1980, when the SEC passed rule 19c-3, which allowed New York Stock Exchange member firms to trade listed stocks off the exchange floor—in the so-called over-the-counter (OTC) market. A closed, private world, the OTC market was a virtual money machine for dealers. Bid-offer spreads remained wide thanks to informal collusion. Even the most actively traded stock spreads almost never narrowed between "even eighth" increments—in other words, 2/8 to 4/8 to 6/8—which works out to a dealer's take of 25 cents per share per trade.[4] Investors complained bitterly about OTC trading costs, but regulators looked the other way, devoting their attention to the New York Stock Exchange (NYSE), where by far the greatest dollar volume changed hands.

All of that changed in 1994, when two Vanderbilt University professors published a paper in the *Journal of Finance* noting the absence of odd-eighth quotes in the OTC. They concluded that this was evidence of implicit collusion among market makers to keep spreads artificially high.[5] Based on this paper, the Justice Department launched an antitrust investigation against the dealers, and dozens of class-action lawsuits were filed against NASDAQ market makers. In December 1997 dealers paid $910 million to settle private lawsuits and in early 1999 they agreed to pay the SEC nearly $27 million in fines.

The SEC also imposed new order-handling rules on all market makers. One of the most sweeping components of these reforms is the Limit Order Display Rule, mandating that customer limit order of between 100 and 10,000 shares that bettered a dealer's price quote must be displayed on a screen. Before the rule changes, market makers could sit on customer offers that they found were disadvantageous. Spreads on many OTC stocks were cut 30 percent in a matter of weeks.[6]

As a result of these changes, mutual funds have dramatically cut their trading costs. Large fund families like Vanguard and American Century have saved between 10 and 20 basis points—or $100,000 to $200,000 per $100 million of assets—as a result of the narrowing in OTC spreads.[7]

This new technology has enabled mutual fund operations to become more efficient in their trading activity, which has resulted in meaningful savings for their investors. But an odd by-product of this efficiency has also been a significant increase in the workload of portfolio managers (the individuals who manage the day-to-day investments of customer assets). The average fund manager currently runs approximately $1.8 billion of capital—an increase of 65 percent since 1994.[8]

As the largest component of the investment industry, mutual funds offer individual investors access to stocks and bonds in a form that is much cheaper and more efficient than if one were to construct a portfolio on his or her own. And since mutual funds have small minimum investments, they also offer individuals the ability to diversify their holdings across a variety of domestic and international markets. Based on these advantages and the unrelenting bull market of the last 20 years, there is little wonder why the mutual fund industry has experienced such explosive growth. Yet, one must wonder if such a huge increase in assets has effected the ability of active managed funds to execute their strategies in the capital markets. Is there a limit to how much customer money a portfolio manager can effectively handle?

As opposed to the large economies of scale that describe running a mutual fund company, there are *diseconomies of scale* for actively managed investments. In other words, portfolio managers have a tougher time outperforming a passive benchmark as fund size increases. These diseconomies occur because transaction costs increase with trading size.

Transaction costs have two components, commissions and market impact. Commissions tend to be small and are steadily decreasing thanks to increasing competition among brokerage firms and the ever-increasing trading volume of equities around the world. Market impact is defined as the difference between an execution price and the posted price for a stock. Market impact can be substantial, and is often quite large at the worst possible time. For example, after the release of a negative earnings report, a company's stock can be quoted "49-50" ($49 per share to sell; $50 per share to buy) by a specialist on the floor of the New York Stock Exchange. If the portfolio manager for a large fund wants to sell a large block of this stock—say 100,000 shares—the bid-ask spread might widen to "47-50" ($47 per share to sell; $50 per share to buy). In fact, the spread may widen so much that the manager may decide that based solely on market impact, the trade is simply not economically feasible (Figure 3.4). The manager is thus forced to hold a position he does not want, which prevents him from using the cash gained from the transaction to buy a stock he does want to own. The profit potential lost from the manager not owning his stock of choice is commonly referred to as opportunity cost.

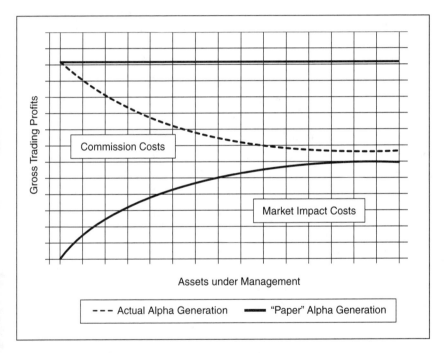

Figure 3.4   Trading Costs

The graph illustrates the difference between "paper" alpha generation (gains made by following a strategy without regard to transaction costs) and actual alpha generation. As assets under management creep higher, commission costs per unit decrease, but market impact (the costs associated with the bid-ask spread on trading) steadily increases with order size.

Portfolio managers use a variety of strategies to minimize their costs under these circumstances. A manager can decide to trade more slowly, for instance. This strategy entails breaking large sell orders into smaller pieces, with the objective of obtaining a better average price for the shares he owns. But slower trading inevitably results in higher opportunity costs, which offset better execution prices. In fact, studies have shown that mutual funds with higher turnover (those that trade more often than their rivals) have consistently higher risk-adjusted returns.[9] Not coincidentally, these funds are often the ones with the smallest level of assets under management.

Some managers, obsessed with the idea of beating the market, take a more pragmatic approach. Numeric Investors L.P., an investment firm based in Cambridge, Massachusetts, analyzes transaction costs to determine the optimum level of assets to manage. Using variables such as the relationship between trade size and trading cost, the firm calculates gross alpha and how returns will change as assets under management vary. Langdon Wheeler, the company's president, explains that increasing assets eventually "consumes alpha" if a fund grows beyond a certain point.[10]

Mutual fund companies are thus left at a crossroad. On one side, they strive to increase the amount of client assets under management to maximize their fee income, while at the same time achieving the all-important economies of scale mentioned earlier. On the other side is the interest of the shareholder, who simply wants the best return possible. It seems logical that investors would eventually shy away from funds that consistently underperform their peers, thereby providing a natural mechanism that would prevent funds from growing too large (or prevent funds from charging excessively high fees). Such a theory would rest on the assumption that investors are rational and make their investment decisions solely in regard to maximizing their return at the lowest possible levels of risk.

Unfortunately, this theory does not hold up in the real world. A recent study in the *Financial Analysts Journal* examined the impact of marketing charges on sales of mutual funds. The results showed that fund companies wishing to increase their client assets under management should concentrate more on fund marketing and service-related functions than on maximizing the return for their shareholders. The study concluded that the majority of mutual fund investors were more concerned with customer services than with financial performance.[11]

α

Besides efficient markets, transaction costs, and fees, mutual fund managers have one more hindrance to their performance—investment constraints. These constraints are generally viewed as a form of risk control. However, depending on the nature of the investment constraint, the resulting portfolios may not be as well diversified and the total level of risk may not necessarily fall. Further, the return-generating process of the portfolio may be greatly hampered. Thus, there is generally a cost in terms of the risk-return tradeoff when constraints are involved. This cost must be measured against the potential for abuse that can occur when asset managers are given more freedom.

The most common constraints for mutual fund managers include the use of leverage (or margin), which entails using borrowed money to increase one's investment. Other common constraints include a moratorium on short sales (selling shares that are not owned, in the hopes of buying the stock back at a lower price and thus generating a profit) and the use of the foreign exchange market to hedge currency risk if foreign shares are held in the portfolio.

Most constraints that hamper mutual fund managers are the result of the Investment Advisor's Act of 1940 and related rulings, which were passed to protect investors against trading abuses. In an effort to avoid these constraints, many fund managers have elected to bypass the SEC guidelines, and instead operate as a private investment partnership. Although this arrangement allows for a completely unfettered investment style, there are drawbacks. The SEC mandates that such advisors refrain from advertising and limit themselves to a small number of clients (which, depending on registration exemptions, range from 99 to 499 investors). The resulting investment vehicles, called *hedge funds*, have attracted more than $400 billion from investors worldwide.

The A. W. Jones Group, founded in 1949, was the first entity to form such a structure. The name *hedge fund* was derived from their strategy of taking offsetting long and short positions in the stock of companies in the same industry, which both reduced market exposure and allowed the fund to benefit from individual companies' specific performance. There is a number of hedge funds styles from which to choose. Strategies run the gamut from market neutral (funds that seek to profit regardless of the direction of any market) to global macro (which actively invests in the international stock, bond, and currency markets). Some hedge funds specialize in specific market sectors, like small-cap stocks or emerging market debt.

Hedge funds differ from mutual funds in a number of other ways. First, hedge fund managers typically receive performance-based fees (which are also referred to as *incentive fees*). This charge typically amounts to about 20 percent of the net performance of the fund over a set benchmark. Incentive fees strongly motivate these managers to generate exceptional performance. For this reason, hedge funds often limit the amount of client money they will accept for fear that managing an excessive amount of capital will dilute their returns. Because of these size constraints, the best hedge funds are often the hardest to obtain.

From an economic perspective, the enticement of an incentive fee is a huge carrot for savvy and successful mutual fund managers to switch to a hedge fund approach. Investment management firms have not been the only ones to lose stars; analysts and traders from brokerage houses and investment banks have also been attracted by the incredible rewards that cannot be matched by traditional fee structures. Considering this brain drain, and the lack of investment constraints, hedge funds yield important insights into the impact of regulation, alternative investment practices, and incentive alignment on performance.

A recent study in the *Journal of Finance* found that, using a large sample of return data from 1988–1995, hedge funds consistently outperformed mutual funds over every time frame examined. Further, hedge funds were found to be uncorrelated with traditional investments in the stocks and bond markets, which would make them valuable additions to portfolios seeking enhanced diversification.[12]

Hedge funds display many attractive organizational features that should help align the interests of hedge fund managers and investors.

Hedge fund managers tend to invest heavily in their own fund; most receive a substantial portion of their pay in the form of incentive fees; and many are general partners with liability for extreme losses. Hedge fund managers also have a significant amount of latitude and flexibility with respect to investment strategies, because they are largely unregulated and attract a sophisticated client base.[13] Part Two of *Searching for Alpha* introduces some popular hedge fund strategies that can be used in concert with a traditional portfolio of stocks and bonds to produce exceptional investment performance.

Chapter 4

Alpha Respite I:
The Case of the
Tempted Money Manager

Logic is a wreath of pretty flowers that smell bad.

Mr. Spock, Star Trek

Kilgore Trout, a successful investment advisor, runs a boutique firm that specializes in small-capitalization stocks. Trout has about $100 million under management, employs three MBAs (affectionately known as his "quant jocks"), one executive assistant, and teaches Sunday school at the local Presbyterian Church. He charges his clients an annual management fee of 1.25 percent (payable quarterly), which seems reasonable since his firm has handily beaten the total return of the Russell 2000 stock index each of the last five years (and with only 75 percent of the volatility of the index). His methodology is to find stocks that are too small to be followed by the large Wall Street analysts and to establish a position before such coverage is initiated. He feels that this niche is successful because of his insistence on thorough fundamental analysis.

Mr. Trout's skill at identifying promising young companies has become increasingly well known in the investment community. He is occasionally asked to comment on the market by the local television station and is a regular contributor to the *Journal of Portfolio Management*. Trout was recently approached by a successful mutual fund family, who had an interest in hiring him as an advisor on a new small-cap stock fund they were launching. Obviously, this would be quite a coup for Mr. Trout. Not only would his client assets under management increase significantly, but his income and notoriety would also receive a well-deserved shot in the arm. However, all is not what it seems. Upon reading the small print at the bottom of his 60-page advisor agreement, Mr. Trout noticed several conditions that were likely to make running a successful mutual fund quite difficult. For instance, one condition stated that the fund company would require him to keep at least 5 percent of the assets of the fund in cash at all times. This liquidity measure would prevent Mr. Trout from having to sell stocks if a large number of investors decide to bail out simultaneously.

And then there's the problem with research. The fund company had made contractual arrangements that enabled the funds' investment managers to receive research reports from major brokerage firms. These reports are paid for by "soft dollars," which entails paying a higher-than-normal commission rate to compensate the brokerage firms that supply these reports. Of course, Mr. Trout's interests only lie in stocks that are not followed by large Wall Street firms, so he does not have any use for these reports. However, he would still be forced to use these same brokerage firms to execute trades, and based on the contract the fund company has agreed to, all of the assets managed by the fund company are forced to pay the higher execution costs. This arrangement would increase Mr. Trout's usual commission costs of two cents per share to about five cents per share.

Of course, the mutual fund organizers want to raise substantial assets for Mr. Trout's fund. In fact, they are willing to guarantee that the fund will be at least $500 million in six month's time. Mr. Trout is aware this large asset base will both increase his transaction costs and limit his flexibility in entering and exiting positions. In fact, Mr. Trout's quant jocks have informed him (after analyzing thousands of the firm's transactions) that trading costs are a logarithmic function of the size of a portfolio. Based on this analysis, a fivefold increase in assets—from the current $100 million to $500 million—will likely result in a 70 percent increase in transaction costs.[1] To make matters worse for Mr. Trout's potential shareholders, the fund company informed him that the management fee on the fund will likely be increased from the initial 1.25 percent to 1.50 percent after the first 12 months of operation. And finally, Mr. Trout sadly notes, with the interests of their sales force at heart, the fund company has decided to levy the fund with a 12b-1 fee of 0.50 percent per annum.

After some extensive back-of-the-envelope calculations, Mr. Trout determined that the additional fees incurred by the fund would be more than enough to eliminate his trailing five-year excess return (or alpha) generation. And Mr. Trout's potential shareholders are not the only casualty—his existing client base will also suffer because of the increased position sizes he will have to maintain. What are Mr. Trout's choices?

Like all good Presbyterians, Mr. Trout is a practical man. He realizes that accepting the proposal as it stands will, in the long run, hurt his business. But he also acknowledges that his children go to a private school, his quant jocks are getting phone calls from Goldman Sachs, and his Piper Twin Comanche needs a new engine. In this case, pragmatism takes the lead over emotion. He decides to use his MBAs to determine the optimum amount of assets to manage.

$$\alpha$$

Active equity managers seek to create wealth through *alpha generation*, that is, by beating a passive benchmark. Because Mr. Trout specializes in small-cap stocks, the appropriate benchmark is the Russell 2000 index, which represents those issues too small to be included in the large-cap Standard & Poor's (S&P) 500 index. The amount of wealth created equals the rate of return in excess of the benchmark multiplied by the amount of assets under management.[2] For the client, the wealth created should be calculated net of all fees. For Mr. Trout, wealth created equals fees earned minus expenses. Thus, the total wealth created is the pie made up of the client's net dollar gain plus the firm's fee net of expenses. The optimum amount of assets under management is determined by maximizing the size of this pie. This is the most economically logical thing to do. The division of the pie between Mr. Trout and his client should form the basis for negotiating manager compensation.[3]

Like Mr. Trout's fundamental stock analysis, the trade-offs involved in determining the optimum amount of assets under management should follow a top-down approach. First, Mr. Trout needs to estimate the alpha generation of his investment process. This amount is best accomplished by determining how his investment recommendations would have performed without fees or trading costs (if the hypothetical portfolio does poorly, the problem is with research, and perhaps only secondarily with size). In short order, the quant jocks determine that Trout's pro forma alpha generation sans costs is a hefty 4 percent.

Armed with this knowledge, and the relationship between transaction costs and assets under management, the quant jocks are able to illustrate the effects of managing incrementally larger client assets on performance (see Figure 4.1 and Table 4.1).

$$\alpha$$

Winston Smith is a professional investor. His family opened its first grocery store in 1947, in a small town in North Carolina. Smith worked at the store in his youth, and after graduation from the University of Florida, attended the University of North Carolina Graduate School of Business. After the completion of his MBA, Smith returned to the family enterprise, which he successfully expanded to include stores in five neighboring

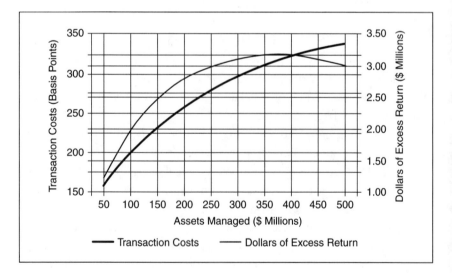

Figure 4.1   **Transaction Costs versus Assets Managed**

Table 4.1   Transaction Costs versus Assets Managed

Assets Managed ($ Millions)	Transactions Costs (%)	Dollars of Excess Return (Alpha) ($ Millions)
50	1.6	1.18
100	2.0	2.00
150	2.4	2.47
200	2.6	2.80
250	2.8	3.01
300	3.0	3.14
350	3.1	3.19
400	3.2	3.18
450	3.3	3.12
500	3.4	3.01

towns. The Smith family later sold its business to a national chain for $20 million. On word of the buyout, the family was inundated by offers from various brokers to manage their money. After listening to countless jumbled and ill-conceived marketing presentations, Mr. Smith decided to shoulder the burden of his family's newfound wealth himself.

Harkening to his graduate school days, Mr. Smith follows a rigorous, analytical approach to money management. To minimize advisory fees, the bulk of his family's funds are committed to indexed strategies. A smaller portion of the family fortune is allocated to actively managed strategies in asset classes that Mr. Smith feels may be inherently complex or underfollowed. Some examples of these niche areas include mortgage-backed securities, small-capitalization stocks, and foreign debt. Mr. Smith has been unusually successful in finding managers capable of generating alpha in these areas. His approach consists of hiring relatively new emerging managers who are quantitatively oriented and exhibit flexibility in fee negotiations. He has developed his abilities in identifying trading talent to such an extent that several other wealthy families have asked him to direct a portion of their assets. Mr. Smith's family office currently manages about $500 million in outside money using this alpha-identification strategy.

Mr. Smith's investments in alpha managers follow a consistent pattern. At the initiation of a new account, performance is as expected. But

as others begin to discover these advisors, the increase in their client assets is almost always associated with a noticeable drop in excess return.
This situation is becoming a problem for Mr. Smith, who has lately experienced substantial growth in client assets. To further exacerbate the situation, Mr. Smith has found that it has become increasingly more difficult
to find promising new talent.

One of Mr. Smith's earliest investments was with Mr. Trout. The two
met several years ago at the local private airport. As a well-connected cit-
izen in his hometown, Mr. Smith quickly learned of Mr. Trout's offer from
the mutual fund family. Mr. Smith became immediately concerned. Faced
with the prospect of losing one of his most successful advisors, he decided
to discuss the situation with Mr. Trout in person.

One of the more potent weapons in Mr. Smith's arsenal is a graph
(Figure 4.2) he constructed several years earlier, when one of his most
promising investment managers was hired as a subadvisor by a bank to run
a large in-house pool of client assets. Mr. Smith closely followed this advisors' track record as his client assets under management increased.

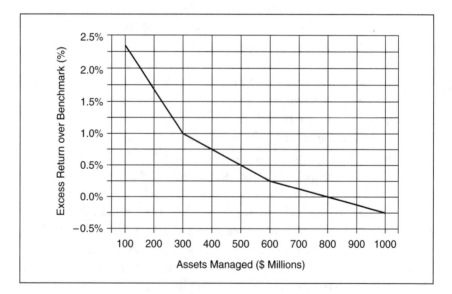

Figure 4.2   Alpha Generation versus Assets Managed

In Mr. Smith's opinion, the relationship between assets under management and alpha generation was undeniable.

$$\alpha$$

From Mr. Smith's point of view, a successful meeting between Mr. Trout and him would address the alignment of interests between advisor and client. Of course, they would both agree that wealth is created from Mr. Trout's investment process. The negotiation between the two should focus on how this wealth should be divided.

One of Mr. Trout's key concerns is the growth of his business. He would like to decrease his dependence on a relatively small client roster, which presently numbers only eight. The withdrawal of any one client would have a noticeable impact on the profitability of Mr. Trout's operation. The mutual fund proposal would reduce his reliance on this small number of clients, and since fund assets tend to be more loyal than individual accounts during periods of adverse performance, Mr. Trout's business would enjoy increased earnings stability. But at issue is the effect of performance on assets. Unless Mr. Trout can expand his niche to include large-cap stocks (which are more liquid and therefore more easy to trade), his edge in the marketplace will have a limited life.

Mr. Smith's concern is with Mr. Trout's incremental alpha generation. Each extra dollar of assets that Mr. Trout accepts will likely diminish his ability to generate returns for existing clients. Mr. Smith is also concerned with possible *style drift*. If Mr. Trout decides to sharply expand his assets under management, he will likely have to change his methodology to include larger stocks that are more frequently traded. Stocks such as these typically receive more coverage by Wall Street and are thus more efficiently priced, making alpha generation more difficult.

If the client–advisor relationship is to stay intact, Mr. Smith must find a way to entice Mr. Trout to limit his assets under management. Mr. Smith's proposal can take two forms.

First, Mr. Trout can offer Mr. Smith a performance (or incentive) fee based on his annual alpha generation. Such a fee would increase Mr. Trout's current earnings. It would also be a disincentive for Mr. Trout to accept further client assets, since such assets would limit his alpha-generating ability (and thus, cap future performance fee income). To sweeten the pot, however, Mr. Smith would likely be forced to increase his allocation to Mr. Trout from the current $20 million level.

There are several problems with this approach. The introduction of asymmetric risk sharing might introduce some additional conflicts of interest. For example, if Mr. Trout is able to generate outstanding performance early in the year, he might be tempted to reduce his positions for the remainder of the year, thus banking his incentive fee. Or, if the first few quarters of the year are disappointing, Mr. Trout might be compelled to take additional risk in the remaining part of the year to boost revenues. Of course, Mr. Smith could pay the incentive fees at the end of each calendar quarter. This would reward Mr. Trout more immediately if the outperformance occurred early in the year, thus delineating the need for him to exercise undue caution later in the year. As for the latter problem, Mr. Smith might consider adding restrictions to the advisory agreement that limits Mr. Trout's use of excessive risk (through concentration in a stock, the use of leverage, etc.).

Mr. Smith might also consider taking an equity stake in Mr. Trout's firm. This unique structure would serve several purposes. First, it would give Mr. Trout an immediate influx of cash, which he could use to improve his lifestyle. Mr. Trout could also use the infusion to develop new trading methodologies, which might enable him to manage more client assets. Perhaps more importantly to Mr. Smith, however, is the prospect of receiving a portion of the fee revenue from the client assets managed by Mr. Trout's firm. This income would boost the return of Mr. Smith's original investment. A stake would also serve as an effective hedge should Mr. Trout decide to accept a level of client assets that might cramp his alpha-generating capabilities, because the additional fee income to Mr. Smith would partially offset the reduction in alpha generation by Mr. Trout.

α

Under his current fixed fee structure, Mr. Trout's income is not directly related to his ability to generate alpha. As Figure 4.3 illustrates, Mr.

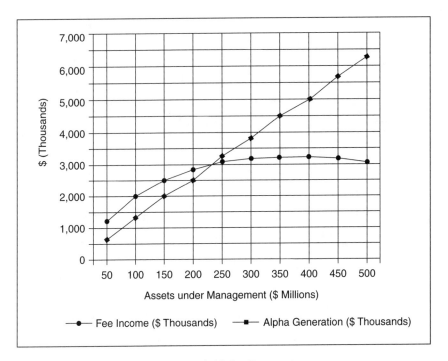

Figure 4.3   Management Fees and Alpha Generation

Trout's alpha generation peaks when assets reach $350 million. However, because his fee income is based only on assets under management, Mr. Trout's revenues increase indefinitely. It is clearly in Mr. Smith's best interest to find a way to link Mr. Trout's compensation to his trading performance in a more direct manner.

Several of Mr. Smith's managers receive performance-based fees. The typical arrangement consists of a fixed management fee of about 1 percent per annum and a performance (or incentive) fee equivalent to 25 percent of the alpha generated above the benchmark. Mr. Smith felt that this might be a fair fee arrangement for Mr. Trout to consider. Even though Mr. Trout would be receiving a small management fee, the addition of the performance fee would increase his overall revenues. Mr. Smith then constructed the graph shown in Figure 4.4 to illustrate the change in Trout's fee income:

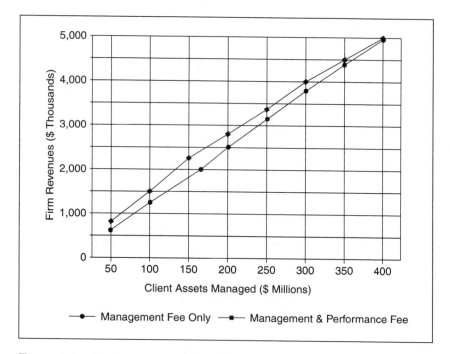

Figure 4.4   Fee Structure and Firm Revenues

Figure 4.4 clearly shows that the addition of a performance fee enhances Mr. Trout's income. Yet, the higher fixed management fee (1.25 percent per annum) exceeds the combined management and incentive fees as assets under management reach $350 million. Mr. Smith is forced to recognize that Mr. Trout's income is maximized not at the point of maximum alpha generation, but at a level of assets more consistent with the average mutual fund manager. If Mr. Trout is truly committed to value-added investment management, it is quite likely that he is limiting his firm's revenue stream.

Mr. Smith's other alternative is to purchase a portion of Mr. Trout's firm. At the current level of client assets ($100 million), Mr. Trout's annual corporate profit is approximately $500,000. According to *Annual Statement Studies* (a publication of Robert Morris Associates), the average

price/earnings multiple for an investment firm of Mr. Trout's size is about
12.5. Thus, the value of Mr. Trout's firm is

$$\$500,000 \times 12.5 = \underline{\underline{\$6,250,000}}$$

Mr. Smith could buy a 20 percent stake in Mr. Trout's investment management business for approximately $1.25 million. Further, Mr. Smith
could sweeten the pot by promising to increase his allocation to Mr. Trout.
Mr. Trout would retain the ability to accept funds from other clients and
to maintain his current fee structure. The income to Mr. Smith's investment partnership from Mr. Trout would consist of two components—the
profit from Mr. Trout's trading (Figure 4.5) and 20 percent of the revenues
from Mr. Trout's firm.

An equity stake in Mr. Trout's firm solves two of Mr. Smith's problems.
First, as alpha generation decreases with asset size, Mr. Smith's return
becomes less dependent on Mr. Trout's performance and more dependent
on the revenue stream from Mr. Smith's expanding client base, thus decreasing the volatility of Mr. Smith's cash flow stream from Mr. Trout. An
equity stake also allows Mr. Smith to expand his base of client assets. With

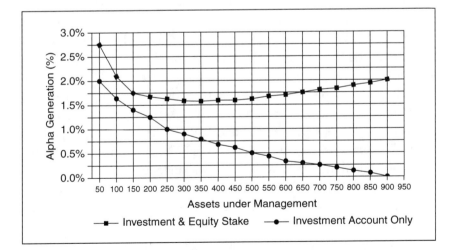

Figure 4.5   Mr. Trout's Alpha Generation (percentage over benchmark)

emerging alpha-generating managers as difficult to identify as ever, Mr. Smith believes that an investment directly in Mr. Trout's firm is an efficient use of capital. The only disadvantage to such an arrangement is a question of taxation; instead of simply dealing with long- and short-term capital gains, an equity stake might expose Mr. Smith's clients to closer Internal Revenue Service (IRS) scrutiny.

α

Mr. Trout's final decision will ultimately be based more on his philosophy than on financial considerations. The addition of a performance fee would transform Trout's firm into something that more resembles a hedge fund than a traditional investment firm. The better hedge funds share several characteristics. First, much like Mr. Trout, hedge fund managers tend to operate within a highly specialized niche. Second, in an effort to maximize their alpha generation, many hedge funds stop accepting client assets when their capability to efficiently execute their trading strategies becomes hampered. Last, in an effort to conceal their market positions, hedge fund managers tend to pool all client assets into a single vehicle. These attributes, combined with the very broad investment mandates in which they operate, have made hedge funds attractive alternatives to more traditional active managers.

The second proposal, which entails the purchase of an equity stake by Mr. Smith, has become increasingly popular in the arena of institutional investing. Typically referred to as *coinvesting*, large pension plans occasionally invest alongside, as well as with, promising emerging managers with limited capacity. Other entities, such as Asset Alliance Corporation, a private investment partnership, and ED&F Man International, a large global brokerage firm, have adopted this approach. This is not to say that the mutual fund industry has completely abandoned the pursuit of alpha generation. Of perhaps 5,000 domestic equity funds, approximately one hundred employ some measure of performance in the calculation of their fees. Most of these have limited the amount of client assets they accept.

Conversely, numerous hedge funds have not effectively limited their client assets. Such hedge fund managers are simply "closet indexers" who utilize the hedge fund structure to maximize their personal income. Mr. Smith considers his role in the investment process as one that must differentiate between funds that generate excess return and those that simply generate excess fees.

Market inefficiencies, providing a chance to scoop up money left on the table by the careless or the inept, do not last long. When they do appear, they tend to attract innovative thinkers to Wall Street. The crowd inevitably follows, and the advantage disappears.

Somewhere, thought Mr. Smith, the next Kilgore Trout is finishing his dissertation.[4]

PART TWO

FREE LUNCH, ANYONE?

"This is the investment vehicle
I think would best suit you and
your money manager."

Chapter 5

Arbitrage and Other "Free" Lunches

Forecasting is not a respectable human activity, and not worthwhile beyond the shortest of periods.

Peter Drucker
Management Consultant

The game known in the United States as *football* is indigenous to North America. It did not have one inventor, but rather evolved from soccer and rugby. One of the defining moments in the development of the sport occurred in 1823 in England. William Webb Ellis, a student at the Rugby School, picked up the ball during a soccer game and ran toward the goal. The rules strictly forbade the use of hands, and many people were outraged at Ellis for breaking the rules. Fortunately for Ellis, his impetuous act became the subject of countless stories of young men who were not afraid to go against the mainstream of society. The event was also the birth of the familiar colloquialism "pick up the ball and run with it." A photograph of the plaque at Rugby College commemorating Ellis's achievement is a requisite in any historical treatment of football.[1]

This unassuming infraction, which occurred more than 175 years ago, is the unlikely origin of one of the most profound mysteries in sports—the recent superiority of the National Football Conference (NFC) over the American Football Conference (AFC). There are various schools of thought of why the NFC has dominated in the Super Bowl. Some are of the opinion that coaching is the critical factor. After all, the winner of the 1998 and 1999 world championships, the Denver Broncos (an AFC team), fields a coaching staff largely from an NFC franchise, the San Francisco 49ers. Before the Broncos' repeat victories, the NFC had won an impressive 12 consecutive Super Bowls.

But the game of football is not decided by who employs the smartest coaching staff. Teams win games because they score more points than their opponents do. This is accomplished by running and passing, and by preventing the other team from running and passing. A team's offensive and defensive capabilities can be examined in three ways.[2]

- Point differential—points scored minus points allowed.
- Yard/rush differential—average yards gained per running attempt on offense minus average yards allowed per running attempt on defense.
- Yard/pass attempt differential—average yards gained per pass attempt on offense minus average yards allowed per pass attempt on defense.

Based on these criteria, the NFC fielded a superior team in 10 of the past 14 Super Bowls. In each case, the NFC team was the victor.

What critical factors are responsible for producing superior returns? Fundamentally minded investment advisors consider both macroeconomic and company-specific information in their decision-making process. In order to outmaneuver their competitors, active managers must be able to use this information to generate consistently accurate economic forecasts.

Consider, for example, one of the most popular strategies of increasing returns and reducing risk: market timing. The classic market timer moves his portfolio in and out of stocks, with the intention of being fully invested when the market is rising and out of the market when prices are falling. Effective market timers profit through the mispricing of assets caused by the incorrect assumptions of other investors about either the direction of interest rates or the future growth of the economy. Thus, a successful timer must have the ability to forecast these economic variables more accurately than other market participants.

Another approach widely used at trying to beat the market is stock selection. When investment managers detect significant differences between the price and the value of a stock, they can buy or sell the stock to capture the differential between the market price and the true investment value for their portfolio. The stock selection process thus involves the ability to accurately forecast either the future earnings or the future book value of a given company.

Although they are markedly different from one another, the key to superior investment performance using these strategies is the same— namely, the ability to generate a more accurate forecast than that of the consensus. To be effective, the forecast must produce sufficient excess return to cover the costs associated with active management. The largest components of these expenses are transaction costs and higher investment management fees. After factoring in these costs, it is estimated that the forecast would have to be right at least 70 percent of the time to be worthwhile.[3]

It should come as no surprise that forecasting skill is highly valued on Wall Street. Market strategists, a common title for economic forecasters at large brokerage firms, routinely earn huge salaries for their supposed ability to peer into the future. Most of these gurus refrain from calling exact market tops or bottoms, and instead prefer to make slight changes in their firm's suggested asset allocation. However, a few intrepid souls have sufficient conviction in their beliefs to predict a massive sea change in market direction.

One of the earliest and most well-known market forecasters was Roger Babson. An 1898 graduate of the Massachusetts Institute of Technology, Babson was greatly influenced by the work of Sir Isaac Newton. Newton's third law, "for every action there is an equal and opposite reaction," became the foundation for many of Babson's economic theories. After contracting tuberculosis three years later, he was forced to abandon the idea of working in New York City, so he started an investment newsletter service out of his home in Wellesley Hills, Massachusetts. Named Babson's Reports (now called Babson-United Investment Reports), the service focused on the statistical analysis of stock and bond issues, and was well received by the investment community. Babson quickly amassed a sizable fortune and gained further notoriety by writing a number of books on such diverse topics as business, politics, and religion.

Babson's claim to fame was his keynote speech at the Annual National Business Conference on September 5, 1929. Having witnessed the dramatic bear market of 1907, Babson was convinced that the same financial conditions existed for another, even more violent market correction. In his words, "sooner or later a crash is coming which will take in the leading stocks and cause a decline of from 60 to 80 points in the Dow Jones barometer." In a burst of cheer he concluded that "factories will shut down . . . men will be thrown out of work . . . the vicious circle will get in full swing and the result will be a serious business depression."[4]

Babson could not have made his proclamation at a better time. It was a slack time for news, and every newspaper in the country was vying for a hot headline. By midmorning on September 5th, every major New York and Boston newspaper, wire service, and radio station had gotten tip-off calls that Babson was to deliver a major financial speech at the conference. Soon Babson was receiving calls from reporters seeking an advance of his text. Sensing that the media were going to give him their full attention, he told callers that there would be no advance leaks.[5]

Press interest grew. Reporters knew a refusal to provide an advance was a strong indication that Babson was going to say something extremely newsworthy. Reporters flocked to the conference in large numbers. At 12:30 P.M., United Press International began to punch out the crucial words of Babson's speech. Nearly every afternoon newspaper in America replated its front page news to carry his bearish message. The effect of his speech, called the "Babson Break," resulted in the third largest point loss ever in the Dow Jones Industrial Average, more than 30 points. Stock prices continued their decline in the months that followed. By the time the market reached its lows in 1932, most blue chip stocks had lost more than 90 percent of their value.

On the surface, Babson's prophecy is certainly one of the most amazing in the history of market speculation. Although it will never be known whether this prediction was the result of luck, skill, or a combination of the two, several facts favor chance. First, Babson had been calling for a crash since 1927. His pessimistic speech was broadcast at a delicate time, when Wall Street had the jitters about the economy and the stock market had been driven up artificially with speculative shares bought with borrowed money—a house of cards that had to collapse eventually.[6] Babson was well known for the faulty logic of his past predictions. *Barron's,* in an editorial on September 9th, referred to him as the "sage of Wellesley" and stated that he should not be taken seriously by anyone acquainted with the "notorious inaccuracy of his past statements."[7]

Further, the methods that Babson used to reach his conclusions were suspect. Instead of relying on market statistics, money flows, and other well-known economic tools, Babson instead created what he referred to as the "long-swing-area method," a system that resembled a potpourri of lines, circles, and squares carefully drawn on chart paper. Just because an unusual methodology is not universally accepted does not mean that it does not work. After all, there was a plethora of economists who, using more traditional means, called for higher stock prices. But Babson's technique broke the cardinal rule of the scientific method—its efficacy was never repeated. Choosing to leverage his newfound celebrity in other areas, Babson's greatest market prediction was also his last. He is credited with starting the first business school (Babson College held its 80th anniversary in 1999), served as National Church Moderator for the General Council of the Congregational-Christian Church Association, and even ran for president of the United States in 1940.

Babson's early retirement from the forecasting game is more the rule than the exception. Of all the gurus who were fortunate enough to call a dramatic market turn, very few attempted a repeat performance. And of those few prognosticators, fewer still got it right the second time around. This fact alone points to the near impossibility of accurate forecasting. In his insightful book *The Fortune Sellers,* William Sherden systematically examined the accuracy of all economic forecasts made between 1970 and 1995. His conclusions are summarized as follows:[8]

- *Economists cannot predict the turning points in the economy.* Of the 48 predictions made by prominent economists between 1970 and 1974, 46 failed to foresee large changes in inflation, economic activity, or interest rates. Likewise, from 1976 to 1995 the Federal Reserve Bank failed to predict large changes in gross national product and interest rates.

- *No forecasting methodology produces consistently superior economic forecasts.* In analyzing the track records of 32 economists, there appeared to be no difference in the accuracy ranking among the different economic schools of thought. In fact, the naïve forecast—simply assuming that conditions will be unchanged from the prior period—generates a *better* prediction than most economists for highly volatile economic statistics such as interest rates.

- *Increased sophistication provides no improvement in economic forecast accuracy.* Forecasters using computer models do no better than those relying solely on their subjective judgment, and those using large models of over a thousand equations fare no better than those using simpler models of only a few equations. There is no evidence that economic forecasting "skill" has improved in the last 30 years; in fact, the record indicates that forecasts have actually *decreased* in accuracy. That economists are unable to predict the turning points in the economy suggests that the practice of economic forecasting is a game of chance, not skill, with few consistently beating the odds or excelling at making economic predictions.

$$\alpha$$

History is replete with examples of those who failed to build on a firm foundation. In the Bible, Jesus teaches that the importance of a good foundation becomes especially critical during times of trial (Luke 6:48–49). The story of the three little pigs suggests that building a base with inferior materials could cause the unfortunate ingestion of the guilty party. This concept also holds considerable weight in the realm of traditional investment management. Because both macroeconomic variables and corporate earnings have been shown to fluctuate randomly, it is doubtful that any approach based on one's forecasting acumen is capable of producing fruit. However, an alpha-generating strategy that is not dependent on forecast accuracy could present a desirable alternative to more traditional approaches.

One technique not contingent on an accurate forecast is known as *arbitrage.* An arbitrage strategy entails the simultaneous purchase and sale of the same or similar securities. Typically, the undervalued security is purchased as the overpriced security is sold. The strategy attempts to lock in a riskless profit as the prices for the two securities converge. Forecasting is not an essential element in arbitrage. Rather, profits accrue to those who are able to identify and exploit market mispricings accurately.

Arbitrageurs are a curious lot. Michael Lewis's humorous portrayal of the government bond desk at Salomon Brothers, where he was a broker, described them as quantitatively oriented intellectuals who were "tall, thin, and perpetually tanned."[9] Leading the fray at Salomon was John Merriwether, who recruited talent from the finest finance and mathematics programs in the country. His intent was to form a team with sufficient intellectual horsepower to spot mispricings in the bond market faster than anyone else.

One of the group's biggest coups occurred shortly after the stock market crash in October 1987, when they sold short the newly issued 30-year government bond and bought identical amounts of the 30-year bond the Treasury had issued three months before (short selling a security is a bet that its price will fall). Merriwether's young professors were not the first to notice that the two bonds were virtually identical, but they were the first to have studied so meticulously the relationship between them. They acquired what is referred to as a "liquidity premium," which exists because traders are willing to pay a little more for bonds if the resell market is a little bigger (in this case, the newly issued bonds were more liquid than the older ones). In the hysteria caused by the stock market meltdown, the premium on the new bonds had bloated. The Salomon traders figured that the premium would shrink when the panic abated. Three weeks later, the group cashed out with a $50 million profit.[10]

This is not to say that arbitrage trading was invented at Salomon. The strategy has been used ever since the existence of trading. In the 1930s and 1940s, arbs used to exploit the tendency for mispricings of stocks on the New York and London stock exchanges. The price differences, which were quite large, were primarily caused by the slow distribution of information inherent at that time.

In addition to having historical significance, arbitrage serves an important economic purpose. Arbitrage activity forces prices together, thereby making markets more efficient. Arbs also add liquidity to the marketplace, which makes it easier for others to buy and sell. But the significance of arbitrage in the price discovery process is often not apparent until the activity of arbs diminishes. This is exactly what happened in May 1999, when Chevron acknowledged its intention of buying Texaco, in one of the largest mergers in the oil industry. In a takeover or merger, arbs typically sell the acquiring stock and buy shares in the target company in an effort to profit as the price in the two companies converge. After the announcement was made, however, Texaco stock closed 18 percent below the $80 per share offer price. Although some shunned the deal because of antitrust complications, a big reason why Texaco failed to rise was due to a lack of assets invested in arbitrage funds. Assets in such funds dramatically decreased following their losses in the third quarter of 1998.[11]

Arbitrageurs are also important participants in the futures markets. A farmer is helpless to the vagaries of drought and flood, but he can protect himself against a bear market in grains by selling his crop at planting time, promising future delivery to the buyer at a prearranged price. This price is calculated by the consensus of traders at the Chicago Board of Trade, who congregate in pits, shouting buy and sell orders. This price discovery mechanism is vital to the farmer, because his hedge is dependent on how closely the futures price follows the cash market price.

One of the most important reasons for this price alignment is arbitrage activity. When futures and cash markets get askew of one another, arbs buy the low price and sell the high price simultaneously, thus locking in a profit when the two prices converge. Thus, in a totally efficient market, futures and cash markets are perfect substitutes for one another (because their prices are identical).

This type of arbitrage is not confined to the agricultural markets. Arbs are active in the Standard & Poor's (S&P) 500 stock index futures markets as well. Most index arbs are members of the Chicago Mercantile Exchange, which gives them the ability to sell futures at a moment's notice. Further, the use of the List Order Processing Program (LIST) allows traders to purchase every stock in the index nearly instantaneously. This strategy is also referred to as *program trading*.

α

Besides the ability to quickly identify and exploit market anomalies, there is one more essential ingredient to arbitrage—leverage. Because the price differentials captured by a typical arb transaction are extremely small—in some cases equivalent to just a few basis points (a basis point is 1/100 of 1 percent)—arbitrageurs must have access to lines of credit to enhance their return. The use of borrowed funds to boost returns adds a number of curious nuances to the performance of arbitrage strategies.

First of all, one of the cardinal rules of finance is that borrowed money must be repaid. Banks and brokerage firms that make lines of credit available for arbitrage firms are quite aware of abrupt changes in markets. Lenders have the right to pull credit lines from arbs whenever they perceive the risk of such strategies to be too great for the interest rate charged.

The best way to describe the risk-return tradeoffs of a leveraged arbitrage strategy is by example. Suppose a friend offered you a game of chance with one six-sided dice. If you roll any number between one and five, you receive one dollar. But if you roll a six, you lose four dollars.

Because of its positive expected outcome, the game has statistical appeal. But because the payoff is so low—an expected value of about 17 cents—you decide to borrow funds in order to increase your profits. So instead of betting in one-dollar increments, you decide to use 20 five-dollar increments.

Your lender understands the nature of the game and is willing to finance your venture at a low interest rate. However, there is some concern on his part that an unfortunate string of bad dice rolls could wipe out your grubstake. Because of this risk, he adds a condition to the game: If three consecutive sixes are rolled, the game is stopped and you are personally liable for the loan.

Because the odds of rolling three sixes in a row should occur less than one time in two hundred rolls, you agree to the terms of the loan. Your hope is that if such a bad streak should happen, you have amassed enough profits to cover the arrears.

For the arbitrageur, a good roll is comparable to price convergence. Maximum profit occurs when the prices of two like securities become identical. In most cases, prices do converge, and the arb makes money. But in the unlikely case of a bad roll—the arb equivalent to prices going in opposite directions—substantial losses can occur. There have been several occasions when prices diverged to extreme levels before finally coming together. One of the most famous instances occurred in the third quarter of 1998, when many arbitrage hedge funds, including Long Term Capital Management, were forced to liquidate many of their positions at a loss.

Like the dice game, the potential gain on any given position (or dice roll) is a fixed amount. But because prices can theoretically diverge forever, the largest possible loss for an arbitrage strategy is not fixed—it is *unlimited*. This characteristic of arbitrage—a high probability of a small gain coupled with a small probability of a large loss—has a profound impact on the return distributions of arb funds (Figure 5.1).

The average monthly return of arbitrage hedge funds from 1990 to present is about 0.77 percent per month (this equates to an average annual return of about 9.6 percent per year). Based on the standard deviation of

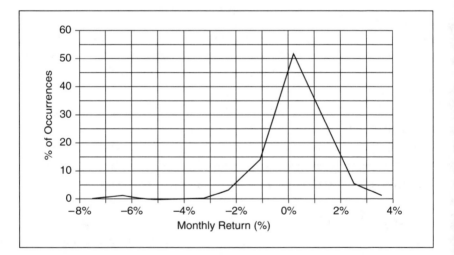

Figure 5.1   Fixed Income Arbitrage Manager's Distribution of Monthly Returns

Arbitrage strategies frequently produce a bimodal return distribution, with many small wins and a few large losses.

returns, one could expect a negative monthly return of more than 3.5 percent every 12 years or so. But in the 8-year period shown on Figure 5.1, there were three such occurrences. Statisticians like to refer to such a distribution as having "fat tails," since large down months happen much more frequently than expected. And when are these unusually bad months most likely to occur? The most common triggers for such adverse returns include sudden interest rate changes and global turmoil. Unfortunately, these are the same types of occurrences that make traditional investments, such as stocks and bonds, also lose value.

Despite their ability to deliver an occasional nasty surprise, arbitrage funds have a large following among institutional investors, high-net worth individuals, and endowments. The strategy can deliver good risk-adjusted returns and is generally not correlated with other asset classes. Few investment styles can deliver consistent performance from such a logical source of alpha as arbitrage.

And there are ways to reduce the severity of bad months. Arbitrageurs are not created equal. Consistent performance is most often attained by arbs that share the following characteristics:

- *Small size.* Successful arb hedge funds tend to limit their client assets under management. This prevents them from having to chase riskier convergence trades in an effort to maintain their rate of return.
- *Specialization.* The best arb fund managers are not generalists. Rather, they act as virtuosos in a specific sector of the investment universe and have developed, through experience, an extremely thorough knowledge of their chosen markets.
- *Reasonable return objectives.* It is much better to view arbitrage as a condiment—an ingredient in a portfolio that offers diversification and a boost to returns—rather than as a main course. The most consistently profitable arb funds are satisfied with an average annualized return of 8–15 percent per year. Those funds shooting for much larger gains either operate in less liquid markets (which are typically riskier and thus offer higher upside potential) or use excessive amounts of leverage. Like all investment strategies, return expectations must be gauged relative to the risks taken.

Chapter 6

Enhancements to CAPM: The Search for Financial DNA

Patriotism stops at champagne.
Otto von Bismarck

In the mid-seventeenth century, the curse of double fermentation—wine that ferments for a second time in the bottle—presented serious problems for vintners. Referred to as *vin diable* (devil wine), the bubbly concoction that was generated caused bottles to explode, sometimes ruining an entire year's harvest. Priests were frequently employed to exorcise the demons responsible for such a calamity from French cellars.

A number of unrelated circumstances arose that solved the problem. The first was the troubling eradication of forests in Great Britain that made fox hunting quite difficult for the English gentry. When brought to the attention of the king, he immediately banned the burning of wood in the manufacturing of glass. The resulting law forced glassmakers to switch fuels to high sulfur coal. Besides creating the infamous "London fog," which killed thousands of people, the use of coal—which burns at a much higher temperature than wood—produced a very strong glass.

Enter a young Benedictine monk in the wine cellar of the Hautvillers Abbey, near the charming cathedral town of Reims, about 60 miles northeast of Paris. Dom Pierre Perignon originally built a reputation as the house's cellarer, in charge of all finance and administrative matters. A cellarer was judged by his ability to increase the revenues of his house by improving the quality and sale of its wines.[1] As such, Dom Perignon did not take well to the idea of discarding wines that had the unfortunate fate of undergoing double fermentation. His quest to improve the profitability of the operation by selling this wine soon became an obsession that spanned a lifetime.

Introduced to English glass by a Portuguese merchant, Dom Perignon reasoned that it might be able to withstand the high pressure caused by second fermentation. The monk also had to develop a sealing mechanism that would keep the bottles tightly closed. The traditional plugs, which were wooden and wrapped in hemp cloth, allowed gases to escape from the bottle. He experimented with various stoppers before being introduced to cork by some visiting Spanish monks. Dom Perignon's greatest contribution to the manufacture of champagne, though, was his method of blending differing grape juices together into a mixture that was greater than the sum of its parts. The *cuvée* method remains the monk's crowning achievement, the culmination of a lifetime of devotion. Eventually, after years of patient trials, Dom Perignon produced the first sparkling "champagne"—named for the province of its birth—in about 1698.[2]

Predictably, champagne's early victories met with some resistance. A few aristocratic gourmets scoffed at the viticultural newcomer, but soon they were overrun by a stampede of champagne lovers. The British Empire soon fell under its spell. After the demise of the steadfast red wine lover, Louis XIV, the French quickly reasoned that Nature made champagne especially for them. Voltaire sang its praises, claiming to find in it the soul of the Frenchman.[3]

And so it is with the capital asset pricing model (CAPM). Although the CAPM was thought from the beginning to be intuitively logical, the number of calculations required to optimally weight even a small portfolio was enormous. It took a series of unrelated circumstances—most notably, a dramatic increase in computing power—to transform the CAPM from an academic theory to the bedrock of modern finance. Inevitably, computing power increased to the extent that financial professionals were in a position to develop an even better mousetrap—a more complex form of the CAPM that did a more complete job of describing the movement of asset prices.

Why was a better mousetrap needed at all? First, the CAPM was developed from a number of simplifying assumptions. For instance, the model assumes no transaction costs. In the real world, such costs often prevent market participants from trading freely enough to price all assets as precisely as they should be priced. Further, the CAPM assumes that all investors are rational. Recent studies have argued that deviations in the CAPM arise from investors following naïve strategies, such as extrapolating past growth rates too far into the future; assuming a trend in stock prices; overreacting to good or bad news; or preferring to invest in firms with a high level of profitability.[4]

But the most important reason for a revved-up model has nothing to do with what the CAPM *is*, but rather what the CAPM is *not*. The capital asset pricing model specifies where asset prices are likely to settle, given investor preferences for trading off risk for expected return. The model states that only one factor explains the risk and return characteristics of a stock—the stock's beta (β). A beta of 1.0 indicates that a stock has the same risk characteristics as the stock market as a whole and should thus earn the same return. A beta of 0.50 connotes a stock with one-half the expected risk of the market and thus one-half of the expected return. Similar to the work of the great monk, the CAPM suggests that by blending various correlated stocks together, one can create a portfolio that has risk and return characteristics that are superior to any of the stocks taken individually.

The noncorrelative property of stocks is an essential ingredient in portfolio design. Yet the CAPM is silent about what makes one group of equities rise or fall differently than another. What was needed was a way to isolate the individual factors responsible for a given stock's returns.

If there was an origin to this type of research, it was the University of Chicago. One of the brightest lights at the Graduate School of Business was Eugene Fama, who coined the term *efficient market hypothesis* in 1964 to describe the stock market's ability to respond almost instantaneously to new information. Fama's concentration in finance was more the result of necessity than destiny. His great love in college was sports, and his major was French. One of Fama's part-time jobs was working for Harry Ernst, a professor who published an investment newsletter. Fama's task was to find profitable trading strategies based on Ernst's favorite stocks. Although he easily found rules that worked, they only seemed to work on paper; when he tried to use them on a real-time basis, they consistently lost money.[5] This experience profoundly affected Fama's views on the stock market. After he graduated from Chicago in 1964 with his Ph.D., he decided to remain as a professor.

Fama is a natural leader, a devoted athlete, and a brilliant rebel whose greatest love is upsetting the natural status quo.[6] Throughout the 1970s, when conventional wisdom held that savvy investment managers could beat the market, he preached with religious zeal at the near futility in outguessing the stock market. "I'd compare stock pickers to astrologers," said Fama, "but I don't want to bad mouth the astrologers."[7] His strong views undoubtedly guided the research efforts of his graduate students. Instead of studying the markets with the intent of finding a better mousetrap, they were encouraged to focus on the characteristics of market behavior.

One of Fama's former students, Rolf Banz, began analyzing the returns on stocks based on the size (or market capitalization) of the company. He found that even after adjusting for risk, small company stocks seemed to outperform the stocks of large companies. Using the database provided by the Center for the Research in Security Prices (CRSP) at the University of Chicago, Banz showed that small stocks—defined as those in the lowest 20 percent of market capitalization on the New York Stock Exchange—generated returns roughly 6 percent higher than large-cap stocks. The excess return of small stocks over large stocks is called the small-stock premium.

Banz felt that the increased riskiness of holding small-cap stocks was at least partially responsible for the extra return. After all, no investor would choose a risky investment except in expectation of earning a commensurately higher performance. Rex Sinquefield, a former student under Fama who worked at American National Bank in Chicago, had been following Banz's research. He proposed that the bank start a small stock index fund; the bank flatly refused. Sinquefield left American National and joined the investment advisory firm Dimensional Fund Advisors (DFA), which was started by a fellow Chicago alum, David Booth. Buoyed by Banz's findings, the first product out of the new firm was an index fund composed of the smallest two deciles (as measured by market capitalization) of all stocks listed on the New York Stock Exchange. The name, the 9-10 Fund, derives from the two deciles. True believers in the efficient market hypothesis, they made no effort to separate the winners from the losers among the fund's holdings. The first index fund based on a subset of the market was born.

Like most investment ideas, the small stock premium is not universally accepted. Some researchers have shown that the return on small-cap stocks can not be achieved by investors because of the high transaction costs in buying these types of shares. Others are quick to point out that the small stock effect is the result of a handful of performance bursts. If one of these bursts is late in arriving, the effect can miss an entire generation.

Others have attacked Banz's conclusions more directly. A recent study indicates that the CRSP database fails to account for stocks that are delisted by stock exchanges for performance-related reasons. The researchers found that CRSP simply ignores these stocks in its calculations, as opposed to hunting down their new, depressingly low prices and computing their returns. The effect becomes even greater in the smallest corner of the NASDAQ. On average, nearly 3 percent of the smallest 5 percent of NASDAQ companies are delisted each month. As a result, CRSP seems to overstate performance.[8]

The results of the study do not completely overwhelm the size effect. It covered only one period (1977–1994), and only one exchange—the NASDAQ. Since Banz studied small-cap stocks listed on the New York Stock Exchange, the research does not directly refute his findings. Further, the CRSP (pronounced "crisp") database is rebalanced quarterly, rather than annually like most other indexes, giving credence to the idea that it is a more accurate reflection of the returns of small stocks.

Of course, that still leaves the problem of transaction costs. The market for small company stocks is thin, so they are quite costly to buy and sell. The estimated trading costs for a stock in the lowest decile of the CRSP database exceeds 3.8 percent. But as the nation's largest trader in small-cap stocks, DFA has transformed an obstacle into an opportunity. The firm's role as a "liquidity provider" in the market—DFA is often the first stop for active managers desperate to buy or sell blocks of small stocks—allows the firm to have *negative* trading costs. Transactions for the 9-10 fund have historically generated about 1.6 percent in profit to clients, which accounts for the bulk of the fund's total alpha generation. Even so, Banz's study is probably the most controversial in modern finance.

α

As it turns out, market capitalization is not the only factor that influences stock returns. Working with Kenneth French of Yale University, Fama found that *value* stocks—defined as those sporting a low price-to-book value ratio—delivered higher historical returns than more expensive issues.[9] According to the study, no other measure was found to have as much predictive power. While "value" managers such as Warren Buffett and Michael Price had long maintained that it was smarter to buy companies when they were out of favor—thus trading at low price-to-book value ratios—Fama and French demonstrated the point with statistical rigor.[10]

What made Fama and French's results so dramatic is that growth stocks like Coca-Cola and General Electric are inevitably the most highly regarded issues, with solid earnings and well-known products. Investors seem to pay for this reliability by accepting a lower return. Value stocks, by contrast, are typically less established but offer greater potential return. The value effect is actually quite similar to the small stock effect, in that more risks pays off with greater returns. In fact, small stocks that also trade at low price-to-book ratios provided the best results. Since Fama and French's work quantified three factors that most influence the returns of a portfolio—the extra risk of stocks versus bonds (the market factor), the extra risk of small-cap stocks over large-cap stocks (the size factor), and the extra risk of value stocks over growth stocks (the value factor), it is most commonly referred to as *the three-factor model.*

The value factor has major historical significance in the investment realm. As laid out in their 1934 classic *Security Analysis*, Benjamin

Graham and David Dodd presented the tenets of value investing as straightforward and eminently logical. According to the authors, investors should buy when stocks have been beaten down and sell when they have been pushed beyond their reasonable values. Virtually all of the great market players of the early nineteenth century, including Alfred Williams, John Maynard Keynes, and Bernard Baruch, all espoused the value approach to stock selection. This should come as no surprise, because the most spectacular market gains should logically come from a stock rising from the ashes. With the combination of academic support, an interesting history, and well-known practitioners, value investing seems to have everything going for it—except that it has not worked in more than a decade.

In four of the past five years, growth stocks have handily outperformed value stocks. In 1998 alone, large-cap growth stocks (as measured by the Russell 1000 growth index) returned 37.5 percent, versus 13.2 percent for the Russell 1000 value index—the worst relative showing for the strategy since the 1970s (see Figure 6.1).[11] Such weak results in the midst of a bull

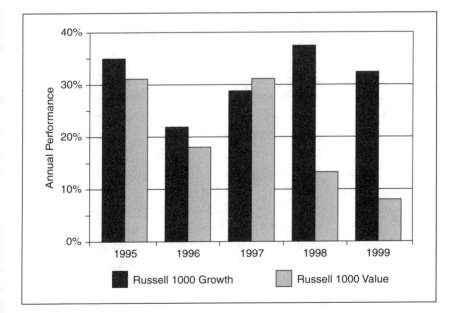

Figure 6.1   Growth Stocks versus Value Stocks

market are not difficult to explain. Each manager has his own spin on the best way to apply the value concept, but in general those guidelines have been directing him or her to buy beaten-down shares in consumer cyclical companies. These stocks have not participated in the narrow rally in the equities market, where only 15 stocks were responsible for one-half of the Standard & Poor's 500 index's gains in 1998.

And what characteristics did these 15 stocks have in common? They are all growth stocks. These "Nifty Fifteen" issues include Microsoft, which traded at the end of the year at a price-to-earnings multiple of 62, and Pfizer, which sports a P/E of 72.[11] In contrast, most value managers prefer stocks with P/E ratios under 10.

True to most styles of active management, the value-investing co-nundrum has experienced alternating periods of favor and condemnation. We refer to this process as methodology preference theory (or MPrT, in order to avoid comparison to the infinitely more important modern port-folio theory).[12] The first step in the MPrT is the discovery of a market anomaly and the subsequent publication of that anomaly in either a book or an academic journal. Other profit-minded individuals act to exploit the opportunity. As assets dedicated to the strategy increase, its efficacy decreases; when assets are at the peak, the strategy inevitably starts to lose money.

The temporary demise of a once-profitable strategy is often met with a flurry of dissertations and manifestos claiming that the strategy never worked in the first place. One by one, die-hard proponents of the strategy lose faith and find other ways to invest their hard-earned assets. At this point in the MPrT process, two outcomes are possible.

The first outcome is the tragic demise of the strategy in question. This occurrence is rather common, as in markets made up of a large pool of professional investors with a tremendous collective pool of research and capabilities. This outcome is even more likely if the anomaly was discov-ered in a more thinly traded market (like high-yield junk bonds or equity options).

The second outcome is the strategy's return to profitability. This out-come is favored by financial writers, who can weave dramatic stories of those individuals who weathered the storms of public humiliation and, true to their convictions, stuck with the system. But even with the best of strategies, MPrT process is destined to repeat itself.

Consultants and active investors can generate a considerable amount of alpha by determining which outcome is the most likely for a given strategy. In general, strategies that have the most chance of renewable profitability have a number of common attributes. First, sustained strategies are typically easy to describe. If a market practitioner uses more than his fair share of Greek letters or 30-symbol equations in his sales presentation, it is best to take a wait-and-see attitude to his approach.

Sustainable strategies are also developed with a reasonable estimate of the costs involved in its implementation. Transaction costs are often higher and more complex than anticipated. Bid-ask spreads have a tendency to widen at the most inopportune times; large blocks of stock are sometimes not tradable at economically feasible prices; and brokers are capable of turning on even their best clients. Alpha-producing strategies that entail a large amount of trading should be carefully scrutinized. Fischer Black, the eminent professor who with Myron Scholes developed the Black-Scholes option pricing model, pointed to the difficulty of turning an academically generated strategy to a real-world moneymaker when he said that "the market looks a lot more efficient from across the Hudson River than from across the Charles."

There are two schools of thought as to why the value approach to investing might have long-term merit. Fama and French argued that because value stocks are a riskier asset class than growth stocks, the market pays a correspondingly higher premium to hold them. This explanation fits well into the CAPM belief that the link between risk and return is linear. And in the 1998 *Journal of Finance* paper "Value versus Growth: The International Evidence," Fama and French extended their grasp by showing that the value effect is present in many foreign stock markets.[13]

The other school of thought shuns the argument that extra risk has anything to do with the outperformance of value stocks. According to Josef Lakonishok, finance professor at the University of Illinois, the catalyst behind the value effect is based on the irrational expectations of market participants. Lakonishok believes that investors are too eager to extrapolate past growth into the future, so that overpriced growth (or "glamour") stocks, which have done well, are expected to continue their run. Meanwhile, expectations for out-of-favor value stocks tend to remain muted.

The real test for any stock is the period that follows earnings announcements. It is common for growth stocks to decline precipitously after missing their profit targets by only a few cents a share. But the pattern is different for value stocks. Like the proverbial lost son, the expectations for value stocks are often so low that even a small improvement is met with enthusiasm. Lakonishok found that value stocks outperform growth stocks in the few days following earnings announcements by a staggering four percentage points. Since the time period studied was so short, it is unlikely that the difference in return was due to higher risk. Lakonishok noted that the results he found were "extremely consistent with the behavioral story, where people are too optimistic about growth stocks and too pessimistic about value stocks."[14] Like many of today's brighter stars in academia, Lakonishok puts his money where his mouth is. His firm, LSV Asset Management, which he founded with Adrei Shleifer of Harvard University and Robert Vishny of the University of Chicago, manages about $5 billion.

α

The search for financial DNA—for a discrete number of factors that determine the fate of an individual stock—did not end at Fama and French's three-factor model. More modern extensions of the CAPM involve anywhere from five to two dozen factors. The origin of this research is a concept known as arbitrage pricing theory (APT). APT was developed by Stephen Ross, a Harvard Ph.D., who was at the time a professor at the University of Pennsylvania (he is now Franco Modigliani Professor of Finance and Economics at Massachusetts Institute of Technology). When Ross originated the theory in 1976, most thought its potential was limited. The main reason was cost—APT required a degree of raw computing power generally not available to the average practitioner. But as computer technology continues to increase in capability, Wall Street has been much more accepting of Ross's ideas.

Both the CAPM and the APT agree that, although many different firm-specific factors can influence the return of an individual stock, these idiosyncratic effects tend to cancel out in large and well-diversified portfolios. For example, an insurance company has no way of knowing whether a particular individual will become sick or will be involved in an accident, but the company is able to accurately predict its losses on a large pool of such risks. However, an insurance company is not entirely free of risk simply because it insures a large number of individuals. Natural disasters or changes in health care can have major influences on insurance losses by simultaneously affecting many claimants. Similarly, well-diversified portfolios are not risk free because there are common economic factors that pervasively influence all stock returns and that cannot be eliminated by diversification.[15]

One commonly used factor relates to the business cycle. If business activity is greater than anticipated, the stocks of companies with high exposure to the business cycle (such as retail stores) should do relatively better than those with less exposure (such as utilities). The APT states that the return and risk characteristics of a stock are dependent on a variety of factors. By constructing a mathematical table called a matrix, APT aficionados can determine which factors are most relevant to a given stock's return.

Matrices can grow quickly in size. As the number of securities increases, the table grows factorially. If one were to measure the risk factors for all listed stocks, bonds, and currencies, more than one billion separate calculations would be required.[16] Fortunately, mathematical shortcuts enable such calculations to be performed on a high-powered PC.

Now recall the basic economic principle called "the law of one price." If two items are identical in every respect, yet priced differently, arbitrage activity should produce an immediate profit—buy the cheap one and sell the expensive one. These trades will bring the prices back in line and eliminate any other profit possibilities. Is the APT exact enough in its measurement of risk that two stocks with similar sensitivity to the same factors can be arbitraged—buy the cheap one and sell the expensive one—for a profit? This strategy, called *pairs trading*, was first used by Morgan Stanley's quantitative trading group in the mid-1980s. Nunzio "Nick"

Tartaglia, a former Jesuit priest and Bell Labs astrophysicist, led the effort. He described the group as "a research laboratory that happens to make money."[17]

This strategy is transaction intensive. It involves making a small profit on a large number of trades. Because of this, leverage is often employed. Most pairs trading operations are owned by registered broker/dealers, who hold two advantages—minimal transactions costs and low borrowing rates. Tartaglia's business model has been duplicated by a considerable number of hedge funds and proprietary trading desks (Figure 6.2).

We have seen how arbitrage pricing theory can be used to compare the risk attributes of individual stocks. The same methodology can be employed in determining the factors responsible for the returns of portfolios. One New York-based firm, APT Inc., uses the theory to design port-

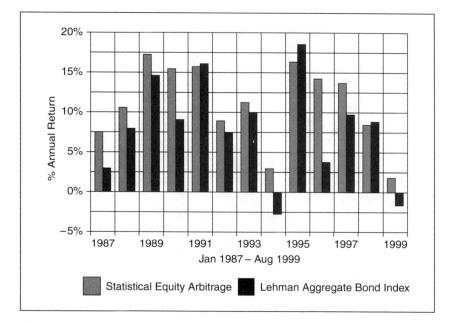

Figure 6.2   Statistical Equity Arbitrage Performance, 1987–1999
Hedge funds utilizing APT-based trading strategies have been able to achieve returns in excess of that of intermediate-term bonds with comparable volatility.

folios to behave predictably. One example is building a fund that acts like the S&P 500 by identifying the index's DNA and replicating it with a mix of securities. Such a replication, claims the company, can be achieved with only 50 different stocks, which would enable investors to create "clone" portfolios with a relatively small amount of cash.

Whether applications like these will convince more managers to convert to an APT-based approach remains to be seen. But as computer technology continues to march forward, and practitioners develop different flavors of the theory to meet their needs, APT may achieve mainstream acceptance within the next decade.

Chapter 7

Managed Futures and Portable Alpha

> One can state, without exaggeration, that the observation of and the search for similarities and differences are the basis of all human knowledge.
>
> *Alfred Nobel*

Alfred Nobel never wanted to blow up *anyone*. Although the famous Swedish scientist is best known for his invention of dynamite, Nobel had a variety of interests, including humanity, literature, and medicine. Nonetheless, the Nobel family made its largest fortune in the context of weaponry. Alfred's father Immanuel gained prominence in Russia for developing naval mines, which effectively deterred the British Royal Navy from invading St. Petersburg during the Crimean War (1853–1856). The elder Nobel was also a pioneer in the design of rockets, cannons, and ammunition.

Alfred met Asconio Sobrero, the discoverer of nitroglycerine, in 1849. Although Nobel was only sixteen years old at the time, he immediately recognized the potential for the substance. The instability of nitroglycerine—it exploded if subjected to heat or pressure—prompted Nobel to experiment with different additives. He eventually found that mixing the liquid with silica would turn nitroglycerine into a paste that could be shaped into rods of a size and form suitable for insertion into drilling holes. These discoveries were made as the diamond drilling crown and pneumatic drill were gaining acceptance in the construction industry. Combined with

Nobel's dynamite, these developments dramatically reduced the cost of blasting rock, drilling tunnels, and building canals. Eventually, Nobel established operations in more than 20 countries.

It was perhaps a by-product of Nobel's global business interests that he became a pacifist. Although his greatest invention was not meant as a weapon, dynamite was used as an explosive in the Franco-Prussian War by both sides. In 1891, he commented that "perhaps my factories will put an end to war sooner than your congresses; on the day that two army corps can mutually annihilate each other in a second, all civilized nations will surely recoil with horror and disband their troops." Nobel did not live long enough to experience the First World War and to discover the error in his thinking.[1]

The uses of nitroglycerine did not end with its explosive properties. Both Nobel and Sobrero had noted that the substance caused severe headaches, although the reason for this occurrence was not known. When distinguished British physician Lauder Brunton found that organic nitrates were effective in relieving chest pains (angina pectoris), Nobel's doctors wondered if a connection existed between the two observations. In 1890, nitroglycerine was first prescribed as a remedy for heart disease. It is now one of the world's most frequently prescribed drugs and has saved countless lives.

And so it goes with futures. Many investors deride futures and other derivative securities because their use conjures up visions of wild speculators that risk all for the slim chance of making a windfall. Trading-related losses are frequently associated with large amounts of press coverage, followed by diatribes by academicians and government officials calling for further regulation of the derivatives industry. But even considering these unfortunate occurrences, the academic justification for futures markets remains strong. The documented benefits to the U.S. economy include helping farmers hedge price risk; allowing companies to manage their portfolios of assets and liabilities more effectively; and providing the ability to borrow in the cheapest capital market, domestic or foreign, without regard to the currency in which the debt is denominated or the form in which interest is paid.[2] And according to Merton Miller, the winner of the 1990 Nobel Prize in economics, derivatives have enabled corporations to deal effectively with many operational risks, including managing the fluctuating prices of raw materials—a risk that has plagued them for centuries. Futures hold equal utility as an investment, and offer attributes that no other asset class can boast. Indeed, a prudent investment in futures has the potential to enhance the diversification of a traditional portfolio of stocks and bonds to a greater extent than other competing alternative investment strategies.

$$\alpha$$

The first recorded case of organized futures trading occurred in Japan during the 1600s. Wealthy landowners and feudal lords of Imperial Japan found themselves squeezed between an expanding monetary economy in the cities and their primarily agrarian-based resources. The rents that they collected from their feudal tenants were paid in the form of a share of each year's rice harvest. This income was irregular and subject to uncontrollable factors, such as weather and crop conditions. Because the money economy required that the nobility have ready cash on hand at all times, income instability stimulated the practice of shipping surplus rice to the principal cities of Osaka and Edo, where it could be stored and sold as needed. In an effort to raise cash quickly, landlords soon began selling tickets (warehouse receipts) against goods stored in rural or urban warehouses. These rice tickets, which eventually became an acceptable form of currency,[3] eventually evolved into the forward (or "to arrive") contract, a widely used financial device in eighteenth century Europe. These contracts allowed for the purchase of goods before their arrival in port.

Forward contracts also filled an important need in the United States grain trade, which during the nineteenth century was subject to seemingly endless cycles of boom and bust. At the end of a crop year, farmers would flood the market with grain, and prices would drop dramatically. Grain would often be left to rot, as prices became so low that transporting it to market became a losing proposition. Later in the year, shortages would develop and prices would rise as dramatically as they had fallen. The use of forward contracts allowed buyers and sellers to negotiate for the delivery of grain at an agreed upon price and delivery date. By 1859, forward contracts had become the medium of choice for the purchase and sale of grains. This was later replaced by the modern futures contract on the Chicago Board of Trade, the first organized commodity exchange in the United States.[4]

Forward contracts and futures contracts share many common attributes. Both allow for the purchase or sale of a specific grade of goods at an agreed to time and place. Futures, however, offer three features that are not inherent in the design of a forward contact:

1. Futures are always traded on an organized exchange. Futures exchanges use clearinghouses to guarantee that the terms of the futures contracts are fulfilled. If either party—the buyer or the seller—of a futures contract defaults, the clearinghouse is available as a counterparty of last resort. In this way, clearinghouses greatly diminish credit risk. In the case of a forward contract between two entities, the risk of default can be quite high.

2. Futures contracts are easily assigned to another party. Participants have the option of taking physical delivery of the goods or placing an offsetting trade at the exchange with another trader. And in the case of futures, buying and selling short (selling with the anticipation of falling prices, with the intent of buying back at a lower price) are easy. A position in a forward contract is typically not as liquid as one in a futures contract.

3. Futures contracts have standardized terms. The quality, quantity, and delivery date of the goods purchased and sold is predetermined by the exchange. This feature enhances the liquidity of most futures contracts, since the terms are generally agreeable to a large number of traders. Conversely, forward contracts are typically customized arrangements between two parties.

Besides liquidity and the ability to initiate short positions, futures boast a distinguishing characteristic not available to holders of traditional securities—inherent leverage. Investors can generally borrow as much as 50 percent of the value of the stock they own, under margin lending requirements set by the Federal Reserve Board. An individual wishing to buy $10,000 of stock can put up $5,000 and borrow the other $5,000, using all of his shares as collateral for the loan. The loan usually carries an interest rate of 9 to 10 percent per year.

Futures trading does not require an initial investment. Rather, futures exchanges make both the buyer and the seller post a security deposit known as *margin*. But unlike equity traders, who can only borrow 50 percent of the money needed to make a transaction, the margin required for futures trading is typically 3 to 5 percent of the value of the underlying contract. And since buying and selling futures does not entail a loan, futures traders do not have to pay interest. So for futures traders, leverage is both abundant and free.

All of these attributes made these newly created financial instruments the vehicle of choice for speculators. By the early 1900s, many large speculators reasoned that by "cornering" a market—which entails owning enough of a commodity to dictate the prices and terms to other traders—huge sums of money could be made. One of the big plungers was Benjamin P. "Old Hutch" Hutchinson, who began operating in the wheat pit in 1864. In 1866 he was given credit for the first significant corner in the wheat pit, a singular honor. Hutch dominated the Chicago grain markets until the early 1890s. But other manipulators vied for the title of "Wheat King" in their cornering operations. One such trader was Joe Leiter. A Harvard graduate, Leiter began his famous attempt to corner wheat in 1897. He was successful at the beginning, until P. D. Armour, the largest short, hired a fleet of boats to bring grain into Chicago. Let by a flotilla of tugboats, Armour's ships broke through the ice on the Great Lakes and delivered to Leiter some 10 million bushels of wheat. Undaunted, Leiter continued to buy, but a river of wheat poured into Chicago from all sections of the country. The corner finally collapsed in "a pit of frantic brokers fighting like madmen." Leiter and his family lost several million dollars, and his membership was indefinitely suspended from the Chicago Board of Trade.[5]

The great operators were legends in their own time. It was said that children often aspired to be market plungers rather than president. By the turn of the century, speculation on the grain exchanges had become a widespread practice by many respectable and ambitious businessmen. John Anderson Truman became wealthy as a result of his speculations in the wheat market at the Kansas City Board of Trade. In 1901, however, in a single transaction, he lost more than $40,000 and was forced to reduce his lifestyle. This included the termination of his son's formal schooling. "I never got a college education. You can feel the lack of it when you sit here. It is a shortcoming," lamented his young progeny. Harry's irritation toward futures traders became well known to the grain exchanges when he became the thirty-third president of the United States.

In 1949 and 1950, increased speculative trading occurred in the futures markets as a result of the outbreak of the Korean War. This trading caused huge increases in the price of grains, lard, cotton, and other commodities. Facing the threat of inflation, President Truman requested Congress to extend the Defense Production Act of 1950 and to add a provision to its terms that would authorize federal control of margin requirements for trading.

But Truman's revulsion of traders did little to quell the speculative fervor of the time. A short time after his request to Congress, a committee began to investigate rumors that members of the Truman administration were profiting in the commodities markets. Congress then passed a joint resolution requiring that the exchanges publish the names of speculators in the markets. President Truman signed the resolution, only to learn that his close friend and personal physician, Gerald Graham, had been speculating in the markets and had made $6,000 in a few months' time. It was also discovered that a special assistant to the Secretary of the Army, in three years of commodity trading, had amassed a fortune of nearly $1 million. He denied that inside information had played any part in his success, but was forced to resign after it was charged by Congress that his "sense of right or wrong was not fully developed."[6]

Shortly after the scandal, the commodity exchanges announced increases in speculative margin rates, which led to the defeat of the margin provisions of the Defense Production Act. Since that time, exchanges have maintained their control over margin rates and have enjoyed great success in preventing unlawful market corners. There have been fewer than five cases of unlawful market manipulation in the last 25 years, and in those cases the operators were not able to profit from their schemes.

α

The era of modern financial futures markets began in May 1972, when the Chicago Mercantile Exchange (CME) began trading foreign currency futures. The collapse of the Smithsonian Agreement, which ended the age of fixed-rate foreign exchange in favor of freely floating currencies, greatly contributed to the success of these markets.

The listing of currency futures was first met with skepticism. These were the first futures contracts listed on financial instruments, and many questioned whether a sustainable number of traders would have an interest in trading them. There was also an established bank forward market for currencies, which many believed made the currency futures markets unnecessary.

Currency futures proved their mettle only a few months after their initial release, as trading volume slowly rose to compete with the popular soybean and pork belly contracts. This was followed by the successful launch of the first interest rate futures contracts on the Chicago Board of Trade in 1975 and the introduction of stock index futures in 1982. Like their predecessors, the use of stock index futures has grown significantly and now boasts a greater dollar volume of trading than the New York Stock Exchange. The increasing use of financial futures has played a large role in the growth in the futures industry, the volume of which is now measured in the trillions of dollars.

The vast liquidity of the futures markets has made possible the development of futures as an investment medium. As shown in Figure 7.1, the managed futures industry has grown from a cottage industry with less than $500 million under management in 1980 to nearly $35 billion in 1998, which makes it one of the larger sectors in the alternative investment arena (the term *managed futures* also includes investments in foreign currencies, which are actively traded in both the futures and forwards markets).

Those who specialize in actively managed futures portfolios are referred to as commodity trading advisors (CTAs), although most of the larger participants concentrate their efforts in the more liquid financial

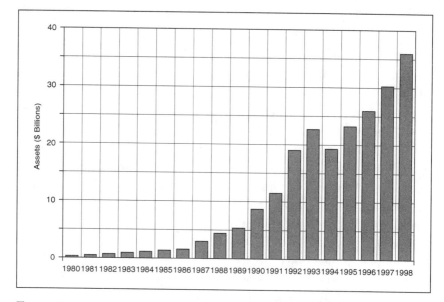

Figure 7.1   Assets Committed to Managed Futures 1980–1999
Source: Based on data from Managed Account Reports.

futures markets. The bulk of assets dedicated to managed futures are dedicated to a strategy called *trend following* (see Figure 7.2). An investor who religiously adhered to a trend-following methodology would be trading in the direction of the prevailing trend in the marketplace. That is because such traders assume that once a trend is in existence, it will remain so until a market shock or other dislocation causes prices to move in the other direction, in which case an opposite position would be initiated.

There are several advantages to a trend-following approach in the futures markets. Because positions are only initiated at the start of a perceived market trend, the number of transactions generated by a trend-based system is modest. Second, trend-based traders often have the opportunity to utilize their methodology in a wide variety of contracts, including the metals, energies, currencies, interest rate, and grain markets.

A wide variety of trend-following rules abound, but they all share the same basic properties of extrapolation. Because these models base their

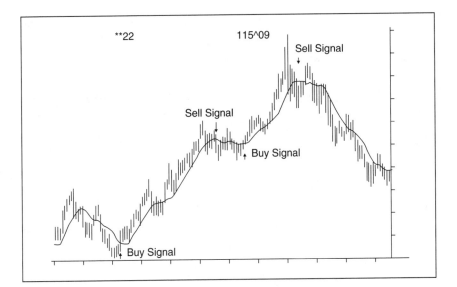

Figure 7.2   The Trend-Following Strategy
Trend followers attempt to enter markets at the beginning of perceived price trends, with
the objective of profiting as the trend develops. Many traders use quantitative tools such
as moving averages to determine when to enter and exit positions.
Chart created using Tradestation 4.0 by Omega Research, Inc.

forecasts on prior price action, buy or sell signals can only be generated
after a market has already begun rising or falling. Thus, a trend-following
approach does not attempt to catch the very top or bottom of market
moves. Instead, it tries to capture enough of a market move to earn a
profit. Profits are possible only if market movements persist long enough
and are of a sufficient size to produce gains after trading costs.

Like all other active strategies, trend following depends on market inefficiencies. Specifically, price trends must be established and then persist
for a significant period of time. But if the existence of persistent trends
were evident, profit-maximizing investors would quickly capitalize on
them and by their collective action ensure that successive price changes
were random. That is, if fundamental economic forces dictated that prices
should exhibit large price swings, an efficient market should discount this

expected future price change into the present—resulting in a large, rapid change in price rather than a series of small price changes. If prices moved in such a fashion, the resulting swing could not possibly be captured by a trend-following trading rule.

Efficient market advocates contend that the process governing price changes in the futures markets (and, indeed, in *all* securities markets) closely approximates a random walk. They contend that any trends that portfolio managers observe are more often imagined than real. Efficient market advocates warn that with enough data mining, profitable trading rules can sometimes be found on time series that are randomly generated. But that does not guarantee that such rules will continue to be profitable in the future. In fact, believers in efficient markets feel that such rules will likely cease to be profitable in the future if prices indeed fluctuate randomly.[7]

There are strong arguments on both sides of this issue, from both academicians and practitioners. But like all debates over the efficiency of markets, one side rarely enjoys a sustainable advantage over the other for a long period of time. A huge percentage of research performed prior to 1993 showed that the inclination of markets to exhibit serial correlation—the tendency for prices to close higher in one day if the previous day's close was higher (and vice versa)—was virtually nonexistent. But more recent work has shown that although large price changes are typically followed by moves in the opposite direction, small price changes tend to be highly correlated. This tendency would be undetectable to studies that focus solely on traditional serial correlation tests, which seek to determine only if a stable relationship exists between successive price changes without regard to the magnitude of market movements.[8]

The most obvious question is the degree of success enjoyed by CTAs. Managed Account Reports, Inc. (MAR), a leading publication in the managed futures industry, has followed the returns of CTAs since the industry began in the early 1980s. According to their data, managed futures have returned about 14 percent per year (Figure 7.3). But attempting to capture this return from selecting an individual CTA is as vexing a task as picking a winning mutual fund based on its prior peer ranking.

A number of other strategies are employed by CTAs in the futures markets besides trend following. Some advisors use a short-term, contrar-

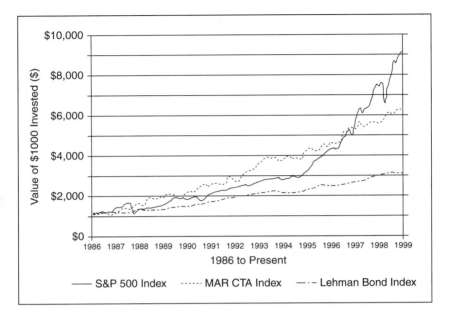

Figure 7.3   Managed Futures, Stocks, and Bonds (value of $1,000 investment)

ian approach, which attempts to exploit the tendency for markets to reverse course after a sustained movement in one direction. Other CTAs use fundamental analysis to determine the long-run direction of prices. Many of the managed futures products that are available for purchase utilize a mixture of these strategies in an attempt to maximize the investment's risk-adjusted return attributes.

α

One of the unique attributes of managed futures is its role as a diversifier. Diversification is, of course, the hallmark of the entire alternative investments industry. If an investment can protect the downside risk of a portfolio and boasts even a modest expected rate of return, there could be some justification of adding it to a traditional portfolio of stocks and bonds.

But investors should not prefer an alternative asset that has only a low correlation with the stock and bond markets. Rather, investors should have a preference for an alternative asset that moves in concert with traditional assets when such assets are doing well and moves in the opposite direction when traditional assets are doing poorly. The statistical tool known as the *correlation coefficient* can serve as a useful measure of the relationship between two sets of data. It ranges between +1, which indicates that two series move in lockstep, to –1, where they are in opposite sync. A correlation of zero means that there is no discernible relationship between the two. For example, the U.S. stock market has a +0.6 relationship with the German stock market; they tend to move together in the same direction. Meanwhile, the correlation coefficient between long-term bond prices and the consumer price index is –0.5, since the two move in opposite directions.[9] In other words, an appropriate diversifier for the U.S. stock market would have high positive correlation with the market portfolio during upswings and high negative correlation during market downswings (Figure 7.4).

Based on this criterion, managed futures seem to accomplish this goal. Historically, the best periods for managed futures are during declines in the stock and bond markets. This attribute is unique among virtually all investments, including other competing strategies in the arena of alternative investments. There have been numerous explanations as to why this is the case. Some believe that market participants act in a more predictable fashion during periods of financial panic. Others point to studies that show that an inflationary environment (i.e., one characterized by rising prices of raw materials), which generally causes lower prices for stocks and bonds, can create pronounced market trends—the perfect environment for CTAs to profit.

But for all of the obvious benefits of managed futures, a relatively small amount of assets is dedicated to the strategy. The first reason is related to the difficulty in selecting individual CTAs for inclusion in a portfolio. Unlike the Standard & Poor's (S&P) 500 index, which can easily be accessed either via an index fund or by purchasing an S&P 500 index futures contract, the broad indices that measure the returns of the managed futures industry are not as easily obtained. And unlike the bulk of equity

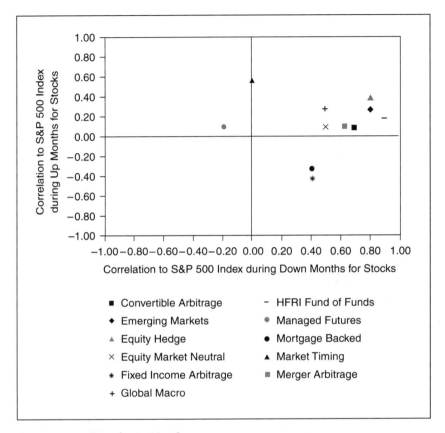

Figure 7.4   **Correlation Analysis**
The best diversifying investment for a portfolio of stocks would perform well during
upswings in the stock market and exhibit negative correlation in bear markets.

managers, whose returns are highly correlated to the S&P 500 index, the
returns of individual CTAs are typically quite different from the MAR
index, or any other index for that matter. Only in the past few years have
indexed products become available for managed futures investors.

The second reason for the small size of the managed futures industry
is advisor volatility. Like investment managers who specialize in traditional equity and fixed-income markets, the historical performance of

CTAs is usually not indicative of future returns. An added complication arises when one realizes that futures advisors do not benchmark themselves to a common index. For this reason, CTAs tend to have different objectives, dissimilar risk tolerances, and discordant methodologies and portfolios. As a result, choosing a CTA can be quite daunting. And if an investor decides to employ a number of CTAs, the administration costs incurred could outweigh the benefits.

But perhaps the biggest constraining factor for the growth of the managed futures industry has to do with the public perception of futures. The benefits of investing in futures and other derivative securities have been widely debated in the popular press. Much of this publicity, while good theater, is often bad economics. Press coverage frequently centers around a few isolated cases in which investors misunderstood the risks of the investment, and it rarely focuses on the broader question of whether a diversified portfolio can benefit from exposure to the futures markets. The situation is particularly vexing for pension fund administrators, who are often skittish of investing in controversial strategies. According to a recent survey, only 27 percent of pension managers utilize derivatives to enhance the return of their portfolios.[10]

α

In the past few years, sophisticated investors have become increasingly focused on measuring investment performance in terms of excess returns relative to an index. This excess return is commonly referred to as alpha (α). In addition to measuring the total return of all investment holdings, portfolios are usually divided into asset classes, such as global stocks, U.S. small-cap stocks, domestic bonds, and global high-yield debt. An index is assigned to each asset class, and the performance of each investment manager utilized in the portfolio is measured on the basis of whether the returns from that particular strategy exceed the index.

Using this modus operandi, both the benchmark component and the alpha component of the return are generated from the same asset class. For example, if investment managers operate under a mandate to exceed the return of the S&P 500 index, they are expected to carry out their mission by actively managing a portfolio of equities from among those included in that index. The total return that they generate—which can be thought of as the benchmark return plus any excess return—is contingent on their abilities as stock-picker, market timer, or a combination of the two.

From a portfolio perspective, it would be optimal if the source of alpha generation were independent of the source of the benchmark return. If this were possible, the return in excess of the benchmark could add valuable diversification.

Investments in futures are unique because they do not require full funding. Because the bulk of CTAs utilize only a fraction of committed capital to post margin, this type of excess return generation can be produced. Referred to as *portable alpha*, managed futures can be used to generate excess returns over any benchmark.

Using the previous example, an investor interested in utilizing the services of a portfolio manager to exceed the returns of the S&P 500 index could simply choose a manager who attempts to achieve this mandate by actively trading among the different stocks in the index. Or, he could hire an index manager to replicate the return of the S&P 500 and utilize a managed futures investment as an overlay to produce excess return. If the investor chooses the latter, the benchmark return and return from the futures investment are sufficiently noncorrelated to add substantial diversification to the total return. The likely effect of this added diversification is enhanced returns when the stock market is going up, and smaller portfolio losses during bear markets.

There are risk management issues raised by using portable alpha. All portable alpha strategies utilize leverage in some form. In the case of futures, of course, leverage does not entail interest costs (because margin requirements are around 5 percent of the face value of most futures contracts, leverage is an inherent and free component of any managed futures allocation). One must also realize the added complexity and record-keeping requirements of such an investment can be daunting. But considering the lack of success of the traditional approach to alpha generation (which depends on the ability of portfolio managers to exceed benchmark returns in stock and bonds via active management), a portable alpha strategy could be a viable alternative.

$$\alpha$$

The principle known as *Occam's Razor* assumes that simpler explanations are inherently better than more complicated ones. This concept is attributed to the medieval philosopher William of Occam, an English philosopher and Franciscan monk. William was a minimalist in this life, idealizing a life of poverty, and like St. Francis of Assisi, found himself battling the pope over the issue. William was excommunicated by Pope John XXII. He responded by writing a treatise demonstrating that Pope John was a heretic.[11]

Also known as the principle of parsimony, Occam's razor underlies all scientific modeling and theory building. For any given model, the theory helps in eliminating the concepts, variables, or constructs that are not needed to explain the phenomenon in question. By doing this, developing a model becomes easier, and there is less chance of introducing inconsistencies, ambiguities, or redundancies.

Based on the extraordinarily complex mathematical forecasting tools used to estimate the future direction of interest rates and corporate earnings (and the dismal track record of economists who use such models), Occam's razor might have considerable merit in the investment industry. It is somehow ironic that for all the complexities of futures contracts, many CTAs base their decisions on a rather simple naïve forecast—the belief that higher (or lower) prices in the recent past will likely lead to higher (or lower) prices in the future.

In the past five years, any investment not connected with the stock market—even those specifically designed to protect portfolios in the event of a bear market—have been akin to bringing an umbrella to a picnic. With the solid gains persisting on Wall Street during the latter half of the 1990s, many investors have simply not seen much risk to hedge against. A severe stock market correction could force investors to reconsider managed futures (and other nontraditional investments) as a practical alternative to their overreliance on the U.S. stock market.

Chapter 8

Alpha Respite II: The Case of the Converging Correlations

> The only thing necessary for the triumph of evil is for good
> men to do nothing.
>
> *Attributed to Edmund Burke*

Winston Smith gazed contemplatively at his glass of 1986 Chateau Lafite Rothschild. The vintage wine was a gift from one of his first clients, and Mr. Smith chose a momentous occasion—the adjournment of a tense meeting with this same client—to pop the cork. Great Bordeaux is a combination of three distinct grapes—cabernet for complexity and elegance, merlot for smoothness and consistency, and cabernet franc for acidity and fragrance. The great wine house of Lafite Rothschild, whose origin dates to 1755, earned a reputation based on its skill in blending these varieties of grapes into a product greater than the sum of its parts. It was this skill that Mr. Smith needed now more than ever.

It is November 1998. The financial carnage of the last several months has taken an onerous toll on a number of Mr. Smith's best investment managers. The collapse of the Russian debt market and the ensuing panic from the disintegration of Long Term Capital Management did particular damage to convergence strategies—those that buy and sell similar securities simultaneously in the hope that their prices will intersect in an orderly fashion. As a result, Mr. Smith was contemplating the first losing year of his multiple-advisor "fund of funds," an investment he feverishly touted as market neutral—able to profit in any market condition.

Mr. Smith started his fund-of-funds program in early 1995. As the general partner (GP) of the fund, he is responsible for allocating its capital to an elite group of investment managers. He selects these managers based on their ability to outperform their respective benchmarks, the uniqueness of their strategies, and the length of their track records. Mr. Smith prefers to hire managers after their second or third year of business, because they are far enough along to have a stable infrastructure, but young enough to show flexibility in fee negotiations. All of the managers hired to advise portions of the fund receive compensation based on performance.

Of course, no product can be sold unless there are entities that are allowed to buy. In the case of Mr. Smith's fund of funds, the opportunity to bring his product to market was significantly enhanced by a 1995 revenue ruling issued by the Internal Revenue Service (IRS) regarding unrelated business taxable income (UBTI).

The story of the tax on unrelated business income began at the end of World War II, when New York University (NYU) Law School formed a wholly owned charitable subsidiary to acquire, with borrowed money, a pasta manufacturer named C. F. Mueller Company. Because the subsidiary was tax exempt, NYU would be able to pay off its acquisition loan with Mueller's profits, while incurring no tax consequences. This technique would have given tax-exempt entities a huge advantage over their taxable competitors in purchasing corporations. Indeed, it was foreseeable that a significant portion of U.S. firms could end up in the hands of tax-exempt organizations and thus be removed from the income tax rolls.[1] Faced with a significant loss of revenue, neither the U.S. Treasury nor the IRS seemed particularly amused at this novel concept.

Under the formulation of the original tax on unrelated taxable income, the income of tax exempt organizations was made subject to regular income tax rates to the extent that it was derived from a business that was not substantially related to the exempt functions of the organization. And since the production of spaghetti was not usually associated with the production of barristers, NYU (and any of its imitators) would be subject to tax.

To further discourage similar financial shenanigans, Congress passed a second category of UBTI—income from debt-financed property. Under these rules, any income derived from a property that was purchased through borrowed funds was taxable.

Sadly, these rules seemed to apply to the returns of any investment manager who used leverage (borrowed money) as a salient component to their strategy. UBTI would also apply to short sales (selling stock that is not owned, with the thought of buying it back at a lower price), a key ingredient to many market neutral equity approaches.

Some of the most important clients in Mr. Smith's roster are tax-exempt entities. Of special note are the many trusts and endowments that he advises. For these types of accounts, if any UBTI is incurred, it is all subject to tax. Thus, the threat of UBTI is quite serious. Mr. Smith also advises a few pension accounts. Although at present a negligible component of his business, Mr. Smith feels that pension assets could represent substantial growth opportunities for his firm. Pensions tend to stay far away from any potential source of UBTI, because of the administrative hassle and the enhanced reporting to the Internal Revenue Service. Thus, the 1995 IRS ruling that specifically excluded both short sales and leverage from the burden of UBTI created a great window of opportunity for Mr. Smith to expand his investment boutique to include an in-house market neutral fund-of-funds product.[2]

Mr. Smith was not alone in his enthusiasm for this sector of the alternative investment universe. Assets dedicated to hedge fund strategies, which boasted an annualized growth rate of more than 20 percent before reaching a three-year plateau in 1993, more than doubled in the two years following the 1995 IRS ruling (Figure 8.1).

Mr. Smith's plan was to design a fund of funds that appealed to the conservative nature of the wealthy individuals and endowments that made up the core of his client base. His intent was to create an investment that would generate annual returns in the low to mid-teens with extremely low volatility. Such an investment, if uncorrelated to changes in interest rates, would make an impressive addition to a portfolio dominated by conservative fixed-income investments and stocks. The strategies employed by Mr. Smith's fund are shown in Table 8.1.

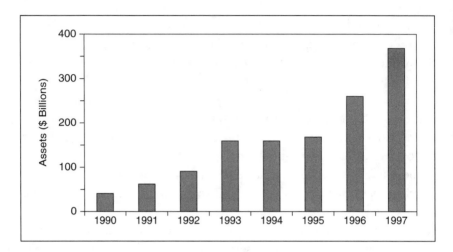

Figure 8.1   **Growth in the Hedge Fund Industry, 1990–1997**
Following the 1995 IRS ruling that excluded short sales and leverage from unrelated taxable income, assets in hedge funds grew dramatically.

The correlation coefficients shown in the two rightmost columns measure the relationship between each strategy with both the Standard & Poor's (S&P) 500 stock index and the U.S. Treasury bond with a 30-year maturity. Correlation coefficients range between 1.0 and –1.0. If two investments are perfectly correlated—that is, if they move up and down in unison—their correlation coefficient would be 1.0. Perfect negative correlation, which would represent two investments that move in opposite directions, would sport a coefficient of –1.0. As Table 8.1 shows, there is minimal correlation between any of the strategies employed by Mr. Smith's fund and the U.S. stock or bond markets. The fund could potentially add important diversification to Mr. Smith's client portfolios.

Of course, the work involved in running a fund of funds does not end with the initial selection of investment managers. To that end, Mr. Smith has developed an elaborate due diligence mechanism to determine if an existing manager should be terminated. Mr. Smith does not believe that a

Table 8.1 Strategies Employed by Mr. Smith's Hedge Fund of Funds

Smoky Mountain Market Neutral Fund LP

Type	Description	Annual Return Expectation (%)	Manager Correlations To	
			S&P 500 Index	U.S. Bond Market
Fixed Income Arbitrage	Simultaneous purchase and sale of similar debt instruments. Utilizes leverage.	14	(0.2)	0.1
Mortgage-Backed Securities	Actively managed portfolio of mortgage-backed securities, on an interest rate and prepayment neutral basis.	10	0.1	(0.1)
Stock Index Arbitrage	Simultaneous purchase of stocks and sale of stock index futures contract.	8	0.1	(0.2)
Equity Market Neutral	Utilizes arbitrage pricing theory to exploit pricing anomalies in the stock market.	11	0.3	(0.4)
Convertible Bond Arbitrage	Simultaneous purchase of convertible bond and short sale of underlying stock.	11	0.4	0.1
High-Yield Bond Management	Actively managed portfolio of high yield corporate bonds.	13	0.5	0.1
Relative Value Currency	Exploits interest rate differentials between currencies.	8	(0.2)	0.3
Event-Driven Equity	Purchases stocks based on the most likely outcome of major corporate events (mergers, bankruptcies, etc.).	20	0.4	0.1
Capital Structure Arbitrage	Simultaneous purchase and sale of similarly rated corporate bonds.	15	-0.3	0.2
Time Zone Arbitrage	Exploits anomalies in the pricing of international mutual funds.	17	0.1	0.0

period of poor performance is sufficient cause for termination. He feels that it is vitally important to consider qualitative factors, including the following:

- *Asset base versus strategy.* Many alpha-generating investment managers profit from inefficiencies in niches of limited size. However, the high returns often attract more investor assets than can be reasonably managed. This often leads to more risky behavior by the manager (in an attempt to keep returns high), or simply erosion in performance.
- *Vanishing market inefficiency.* Certain managers capitalize on a limited number of inefficiencies. As more capital is devoted to these strategies, inefficiencies are often eliminated, resulting in lower returns.
- *Abrupt change in strategy.* Shifting course certainly undercuts the meaningfulness of past performance, and the basis for investing may no longer exist.
- *Exceeding stated risk parameters.* This can be caused either by unusual market conditions or manager instability.

The result of Mr. Smith's ability to choose talented investment managers and his careful attention to detail has caused him to exceed his annual return targets. He has also managed to beat his benchmark, the Hedge Fund Research Fund-of-Funds index, since inception (Figure 8.2).

α

Proponents of chaos theory believe that there is a hidden pattern to data that appears to be random. Some even believe an event as benign as the flapping of a butterfly's wings can impact global weather patterns. These "chaologists" had a field day in August 1998, when the world's most liquid stock index, the S&P 500, fell nearly 15 percent. What could cause such a calamity? Ironically, it was a country 10 time zones away, with an economy the size of that of the state of Rhode Island, that initiated, in the words of U.S. Treasury Secretary Robert Rubin, "the worst financial crisis in 50 years."

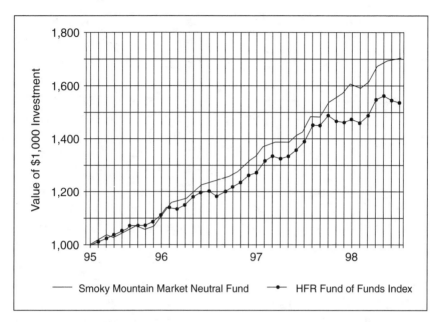

Figure 8.2   Smoky Mountain Market Neutral Fund (net asset value 4/95 to 6/98)

It all started in Thailand. For much of the early 1990s, Thailand boasted one of the highest growth rates in the world. Its rapidly expanding economy was built in part on heavy investment in real estate—shopping malls, office buildings, and condominiums—financed by borrowings from abroad. And like many other Asian countries, Thailand also profited from its substantial export surplus. Many large U.S. corporations invested in the country's infrastructure and built plants to manufacture a wide variety of goods including computer circuit boards and clothing.

The first sign of trouble was the bursting of Thailand's property bubble. Much like the United States in the late 1980s and Japan in the early 1990s, the real estate correction left banks saddled with billions of dollars in bad loans. Many analysts shrugged off the real estate problems, pointing to the country's healthy grow rate. But officials of the International Monetary Fund (IMF) began getting concerned 12 months earlier, when Thailand's currency policies ran aground. Bangkok had tightly linked their currency (the baht) to the U.S. dollar, and up until 1995, that policy helped spur exports because with the dollar generally weak, Thai products sold cheaply on world markets. But then the dollar began to soar, lifting the baht with it. Thai exports became expensive and lost favor in the international marketplace.

In July 1997, Thai authorities vacillated when the IMF privately exhorted them to take actions aimed at boosting exports, such as decoupling the baht from the dollar. Instead, the government made a bad situation even worse by losing billions of dollars in a vain attempt to prop up the baht against speculators betting on a devaluation.

As the baht quickly lost more than 20 percent of its value, other Asian economies fell into the vortex. The prime minister of Malaysia, Dr. Mahathir Mohamad, blamed speculators for the exigency. He was particularly rancorous toward George Soros, at the time the world's largest hedge fund manager, claiming that behind the speculations lay a "Jewish agenda" to return the developing nations into colonial status. The Malaysian government threatened to treat currency trading as a capital offense, banned short sales on the Kuala Lumpur Stock Exchange, and later introduced currency controls.[3] Even after it was discovered that Soros's funds were not carrying short positions in Asian currencies, the Prime Minister refused to retract his earlier statements.

The next 12 months further intensified the crisis. In late October 1997, the Hong Kong stock market lost more than one-quarter of its value on fears over interest rates and pressures on the Hong Kong dollar. South Korea shares also plummeted. Treasury Secretary Rubin urged Tokyo to shore up the Japanese banking system after a number of banks filed for bankruptcy. On August 8, 1998, deepening gloom about the Japanese economy sent the yen tumbling to an eight-year low and stock markets plunged around the world in a dramatic display of financial contagion.

And then there was Russia. On August 17, 1998, Russia defaulted on its sovereign debt. European banks had bought the country's high-risk short-term notes in the belief that Russia was "too big to fail." These investors envisioned a sort of conjectural guarantee in which either the IMF or World Bank would rush to Russia's side in the event of an economic calamity. The belief in this notional insurance policy was so widespread that many institutions had used borrowed funds to buy the Russian debt.

At this point, the world's financial markets lost their composure. If Russia could default, the possibility of other emerging countries following suit became terrifying. The result was a corporate financial panic that threatened to consume the world's largest financial institutions. This series of events culminated in a global rush to liquidity, and the largest bank run in history.

It is difficult to overestimate the importance of Long Term Capital Management (LTCM) in the crisis. As one of the world's largest hedge funds, it held massive arbitrage positions in the global fixed income markets. When their credit lines were pulled, the fund was forced to liquidate these positions at huge losses. And once LTCM's losses became known, many other arbitrage funds were also given margin calls. Unfortunately, most arb funds had either exactly the same or similar positions to LTCM. This further strained the markets, as a plethora of sellers and few buyers can only result in one thing—lower prices.

But perhaps LTCM's most important role was as a scapegoat. The saga was eerily similar to Mary Shelley's *Frankenstein*—a handful of brilliant, Nobel prize-winning economists start a private investment partnership, only to be pummeled to death by the markets that they helped to create. It was, in short, a reporter's dream. Anchors on CNN began to use "Long Term" the way weathermen used El Niño—to justify whatever bizarre event was currently happening in the market. Every day a newspaper or magazine would publish something about the fund that left it more exposed than ever to those that might prey on it. "Every rumor about the size of our positions was always double the truth," said Richard Leahy, a partner in the firm. "Except the rumor about the size of our position in Danish mortgages. That was 10 times what we actually had."[4] These inflated rumors only intensified the situation. And huge losses reported by some of the world's largest investment banking houses—Merrill Lynch, United Bank of Switzerland, and Salomon Brothers, just to name a few—added further fuel to the flames of panic.

Eventually, of course, the convergence trades that LTCM and other funds had wagered on worked out—in the long run. But in this case, the short run became much more important. The use of leverage forced the liquidation of these trades, not the trades themselves.

α

Two aspects of the financial turmoil continued to pester Mr. Smith. The first was the timing of the losses. Market neutral investments earn their stripes by profiting during periods when traditional investments like equities and bonds are falling in value. Mr. Smith noted that the last time market neutral funds experienced adverse conditions was 1994—a difficult year for the stock market. He wanted to know if the two setbacks were somehow connected to one another, and if it was possible to "de-link" his fund from the general direction of the stock market.

The second problem that bothered Mr. Smith was the sheer magnitude of Smoky Mountain's losses. Of course, it is perfectly reasonable to lose money in a market that has lost all composure. But his hand-picked group of advisors managed to lose one and one-half times more than the fund's benchmark. Mr. Smith wanted to determine if the recent underperformance of the fund in the third quarter of 1998 was somehow related to the historical superior returns of the fund since its inception. It was time for his team of quant jocks to spring into action.

α

Bill Watterson is the creator of Calvin and Hobbes, an engaging chronicle of a six-year-old's psyche, which appeared in more than 2,400 newspapers when it ceased publication January 1, 1996. Since it was first syndicated in 1985, Calvin and Hobbes gained worldwide appeal. More than 23 million Calvin and Hobbes books are in print, and each of the 14 book collections has been a million-seller within the first year of publication.

The main character of the strip is named after the stern Protestant theologian of Geneva, John Calvin. A mischievous, self-indulgent boy, Calvin exemplifies the consequences of embracing a purely hedonistic lifestyle. He is an engine of self-interest without the interior governor supplied by a long-term horizon.[5]

Calvin is similar to many who aspire to join the ranks of active investment management. "I am destined for greatness," he says. "Calvin the

Great, they'll call me." He achieves fame in his fantasy life as either Stu-pendous Man or Spaceman Spiff, but in real life he does nothing that would earn him the notoriety he craves. So how does Calvin plan to achieve his objective? The answer, of course, is to be on television. According to Calvin, "I think life should be more like TV. All of life's problems solved within thirty minutes with simple homilies." In that world, "All of our desires should be instantly gratified. Women should always wear tight clothes, and men should carry powerful handguns."[6]

Calvin's best friend is a stuffed tiger. Named after the relentlessly utilitarian British philosopher Thomas Hobbes, Calvin's Hobbes has "the patient dignity and common sense" of most animals the creator of the strip has known.[7] Interestingly, Mr. Watterson thinks of Hobbes neither as a doll that miraculously comes to life when Calvin comes around nor as a product of Calvin's imagination. Rather, Watterson shows "two versions of reality, and each makes complete sense to the participant who sees it."

In this way, Hobbes the tiger has much in common with the myriad of actively managed alternative investment products. It is common for fund managers to have a much different view of their investment vehicle than the actual investor. Much of the difference lies in the benchmark used to evaluate the fund's performance. If the investor is looking to exceed the return of the S&P 500 index, and the manager is happy to deliver 10 percent per annum with low volatility, a divorce is imminent.

The selection of an appropriate benchmark is especially important for "absolute return" managers. These advisors strive to maintain their annual returns in a narrow band (say, 10–15 percent) while assuming the lowest possible risk. And since these managers expect to make this return every year, it is natural for investors to assume that their strategies are independent to the movement of either the stock or bond markets. This mindset is often supported by the manager.

At issue is the plausibility of this assumption. In this case, the asset allocation methodology developed by the manager is of vital importance. If the manager decides on an "accounting-based" approach to market neutrality, where for each asset class long positions are equal in size to short positions, two problems will soon surface. The first problem involves the ever-changing correlations of the assets in the portfolio. Financial instruments have the odd characteristic of acting similarly, especially in a rising interest rate environment. In the second quarter of 1994, for example, following a rise in U.S. interest rates, many market neutral mortgage-backed securities portfolios suffered heavy losses and a few went bankrupt. Still, a few funds that were truly interest-rate neutral managed to hit their return targets, while the market for mortgage-backed securities was suffering from severe distress.[8]

The second problem introduced by the accounting-based approach to market neutrality has to do with liquidity. Limited liquidity goes hand in hand with converging correlations.[9] And both of these conditions are frequently associated with an increase in volatility. These conditions tend to affect managers that operate in the same markets in similar ways. For instance, two arbitrage managers may use totally different methodologies to trade in the domestic fixed income markets. They may never have the same positions, and their performance may be totally uncorrelated. But in the conditions just described, their two shared characteristics—the use of borrowed funds and their exposure to the U.S. bond market—will cause their returns to become highly linked. It is likely in this circumstance that the linkage will cause both managers to lose money.

$$\alpha$$

Mr. Smith's quant jocks tend to view life from a probabilistic point of view. There could be several factors responsible for their perspective. They could simply be right-brained (two of Mr. Smith's three analysts are left-handed), or it could be due to environmental factors (two are males), or simply a result of their academic backgrounds. Two of his analysts have degrees in engineering and mathematics. The other was a former securities analyst for a major Wall Street firm. Regardless of the cause, Mr. Smith's quant jocks are used to delivering concrete answers to the questions that are asked of them. After all, statisticians rarely use the words "maybe" or "sometimes."

The first order of business was to determine how differing market conditions affected the performance of the fund's advisors. Because Smoky

Mountain had only existed in an environment of low interest rates and rising stock prices, there had never been a period where its performance could be compared to crisis periods for equities and fixed income investments. For this reason, the quant jocks decided to include advisor returns prior to the inception of Smoky Mountain in their analysis.

The results alarmed them (Table 8.2). It seemed that the managers employed in the fund performed well and were good alternatives to the stock market—*as long as stocks were appreciating in value.* When stocks were declining, the correlation between stocks and the fund's managers increased significantly. And that is exactly what Mr. Smith's investors do not want.

Although the numbers generated from the quant jock's study seemed to confirm their worst assumptions, they found themselves incapable of making any definitive conclusions. The main reason was the limited amount of data used in the study. Since there were so few hedge fund managers in existence prior to 1994, the quant jocks were forced to begin their analysis at that date. Thus, the study was confined to only 60 months

Table 8.2   Historical Performance of Investment Managers Selected by Smoky Mountain Market Neutral Fund LP, 1994–1998

	Average Monthly Return (%)	
Strategy	When the S&P 500 Is Up	When the S&P 500 Is Down
Fixed Income Arbitrage	2.15	−1.50
Mortgage-Backed Securities	1.46	−0.75
Stock Index Arbitrage	0.65	0.70
Equity Market Neutral	1.50	−0.60
Convertible Bond Arbitrage	1.60	−1.00
High-Yield Bond Management	1.16	−0.25
Relative Value Currency	0.50	0.90
Event-Driven Equity	1.10	−0.52
Capital Structure Arbitrage	2.70	−2.20
Time Zone Arbitrage	2.20	−0.50
HFR Fund-of-Funds Index	**1.40**	**−0.60**
Smoky Mountain Market Neutral Fund	**2.20**	**−0.90**

of returns, with only 14 of those negative months for the S&P 500 index. With such a small sample size, the quant jocks were unwilling to definitively link the recent performance blip of Smoky Mountain to the downdraft in the stock market, or to speculate that a future bear market for equities would adversely effect the fund's performance.

The other issue was the large losses realized by the fund in the third quarter. Smoky Mountain lost more than 18 percent during the Asian crisis, compared to an 11 percent loss for the HFR Fund-of-Funds Index. Mr. Smith was keen on determining if the fund's managers were operating at higher leverage (i.e., they used more borrowed funds) than the average trader in the HFR index. If Mr. Smith's managers were accessing more borrowed funds than their peers, it would explain not only their underperformance in the third quarter, but their overperformance in the period prior to July 1998.

The quant jocks encountered several obstacles in determining the level of leverage utilized by Smoky Mountain's investment managers. First, the managers were hesitant to disclose their positions for fear that the information could be used by their competitors. Even though Mr. Smith's analysts were willing to sign affidavits stating that they would not divulge anything proprietary, the managers remained tightlipped. The limited information that they received was not sufficient to answer Mr. Smith's question. It was at this moment that the quant jocks realized that value of their analysis had hit a wall.

$$\alpha$$

Mr. Smith's circumstance reminded him of the predicament experienced by Roberto della Griva, the young Italian nobleman and main character in Umberto Eco's classic book *The Island of the Day Before*. Roberto was sent by Cardinal Mazarin of France as a spy on a Dutch ship to discover the *Punto Fijo*, the secret of longitude. While latitude can easily be calculated by way of celestial navigation, longitude depends on one's distance from an essentially arbitrary line drawn around the earth (the current meridian goes through Greenwich, Great Britain). And without an accurate clock, there is no way to fix a position exactly—a big quandary for the imperial navies at the time. Longitude was not solved until the invention of the chronometer in 1714.

After the Dutch ship is lost, Roberto finds refuge on an abandoned ship called the *Daphne*. The *Daphne* is full of strange wonders and a myriad of clocks, suggesting that this ship was also looking for the meridian. He also discovers a machine on board that seeks to assemble thousands of atoms of concepts into categories. This machine represents the eternal human need to organize and categorize experience.

Finding himself in a totally foreign environment and lacking a personal point of reference—a personal "meridian," in a sense—Roberto discovers that he cannot organize his thoughts in a manner consistent with the machine's. He finds that knowledge is "a vast ocean of meaning, from which only fleeting allegories and colorful bits of truth can be drawn."[10]

In an environment sufficiently void of information that statistics is of limited use, Mr. Smith knows that his quant jocks have no meridian. Even though the analysts could not come up with a salient conclusion to the fund's problems, Mr. Smith feels that the limited amount of data they compiled was still useful—when combined with experience.

Like the computing device on the *Daphne*, Mr. Smith's first task is to divide Smoky Mountain's portfolio into categories based on manager style. The differences in style weightings between the fund and its benchmark will likely explain the variation in performance between the two investments.

$$\alpha$$

On first glance, Mr. Smith's fund seems more diversified than the index. The factor sensitivity analysis shows that three styles—stock index arbitrage, high yield bonds, and time zone arbitrage—are likely not represented in the average multiadvisor hedge fund. Mr. Smith also notes that these three areas have experienced unusually high profitability in the last year, which could account for the superior returns of Smoky Mountain prior to August 1998.

Mr. Smith next observes the three areas where his fund has more exposure than the index. Fixed income arbitrage, mortgage-backed securities, and capital structure arbitrage represent a higher percentage of Smoky

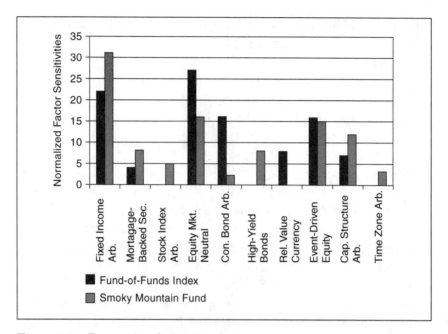

Figure 8.3   **Return Attribution Analysis**

Mountain's returns than his average competitor (Figure 8.3). This is a troubling development. Since these three styles tend to be highly sensitive to changes in interest rates, it is highly probable that the fund's relative overexposure to these areas had a lot to do with the recent losses. Even though Mr. Smith had diversified well with regard to style, he had not done so with regard to economic factors such as interest rate changes, volatility, and limited liquidity.

Mr. Smith knew that his conclusions would be challenged by his quant jocks. First, he had performed the study with limited data. Further, one could probably argue that the "styles" used in the factor analysis were not totally independent (meaning that there were some hedge fund strategies that shared similar sensitivity to changes in macroeconomic conditions). However, the most important conclusion of the exercise was so elementary—namely, that Smoky Mountain's portfolio weightings should be more in line with that of its benchmark—that the lack of complete quantitative verification was a moot point.

Finally, Mr. Smith was aware of only a few fund-of-fund managers who utilized managed futures in their portfolios. The inclusion of the strategy might provide an effective shock absorber for the fund during the next global crisis.

PART III

THE BUSINESS OF ADDING VALUE

"Well, SuperAlpha Man,
you've come to the right place."

Chapter 9

Alpha Generation and Taxes

Don't look back—something may be gaining on you.

Satchel Paige

Monkeys display remarkably humanlike behavior. But despite their innate intelligence, they are surprisingly easy to capture. Monkey-catchers start with a gourd, in which a small hole is drilled and baited with rice. When a monkey plunges his hand in the hole to retrieve the prize, he quickly realizes that the hole is too small for him to remove his rice-filled fist. The monkey thus finds himself in a dilemma—he can either continue his quest for a full stomach, or simply recognize the trap for what it is and run to safety. Unfortunately, most monkeys choose to ignore the long-term consequences of their actions and instead focus on the short term, ending up either as a meal or a weekday special at the local pet shop.

Such is the case with both investors and investment managers regarding taxes. Although both academics and practitioners have spent considerable effort in seeking to create more efficient portfolios, these efforts have largely ignored the long-term effects of taxes on total return. Taxes are frequently the largest expense that many investors face—surpassing both commissions and investment management fees—yet there have been fewer than a dozen published studies that examine its effects on investor wealth. Richard Brealey, a professor at the London Business School and one of the few commentators on the subject, remarks that "return is likely to depend far more on the risk the fund assumes and more on its tax liability than on the accuracy of analysts' forecasts."[1]

An intriguing aspect of taxes is that they are generated by the same mechanism used by investment professionals to enhance returns—active management. Money managers sell one security and buy another solely because they think such activity will result in a higher return than by simply holding a static portfolio. But the true measure of a portfolio's value is obtained only after considering the taxable consequences of capital gains realized by exiting a profitable position.

The recent tax law changes—namely, the Taxpayer Relief Act of 1997—added considerable incentives for U.S. investors to focus on the effects of taxes on returns. Of special note was the reduction in taxes for holding periods of more than five years, which was reduced from 28.0 percent to 18.0 percent (see Table 9.1).

Considering the significant reductions in taxes on securities held for more than one year, one might assume that money managers would have become more tax sensitive. But since the tax law changes, there is no evidence to suggest that the frequency that stocks are bought and sold in

Table 9.1   **Effect of the Taxpayer Relief Act of 1997 on Investment Holdings**

	Effective Tax Rate (%)	
Holding Period	Prior to Enactment	After Enactment
Short Term Less than 12 months	39.6	39.6
Medium Term 12–18 Months	28.0	28.0
Long Term More than 18 months	28.0	20.0
Extra Long Term More than 5 years	28.0	18.0

Source: Internal Revenue Service.

professionally managed portfolios has decreased. This is especially true for stock mutual funds.

Of course, the problem does not rest entirely on the shoulders of fund managers. A fund's tax efficiency is also affected by shareholder purchases and sales. Every year, a fund has to distribute to investors all dividends and capital gains realized in the previous 12 months. If a lot of money flows into the fund from new investors, it dilutes the size of a fund's year-end distribution, which makes the fund seem more tax efficient. Conversely, if investors bail out, the fund may have to sell stocks to pay off these departing shareholders, thus realizing capital gains and generating big taxable distributions for the remaining investors.[2]

But even taking into account the purchases and sales of shareholders, portfolio managers have a number of quantitative tools available to maximize their after-tax performance. And since taxable investors—the investments of individuals, insurance companies, and holding companies, to name a few—account for more than one-half of total investment holdings in the United States, it would seem to be sensible to pursue such strategies.

The most important distinction to make in any tax analysis is the difference between realized and unrealized capital gains. Capital gains are realized when a security is sold and the sale results in a gain in the investor's portfolio. Depending on the length of time the security is held, a tax liability is accrued and must be paid at year's end. Conversely, unrealized capital gains are that part of the portfolio's growth that have not been "cashed in," and thus have not been lessened by taxes. The longer these gains remain unrealized, the more valuable they become, simply due to the effect of tax-free compounding.

It follows that if an active manager's strategy entails the frequent buying and selling of stock, the excess return (or alpha) of this strategy must exceed the tax liability incurred. To determine how portfolio activity, taxes, and alpha generation are linked, we assume an investor has a 10-year investment horizon in an environment where equities are returning approximately 15 percent per annum. The degree of manager activity is measured by the amount of *portfolio turnover*. For example, 50 percent turnover represents that at year's end, one-half of the securities in a portfolio are replaced with new positions. And finally, in our analysis we assume an average capital gains tax rate of 35 percent (Figure 9.1).

The degree with which taxes affect an actively managed portfolio is quite astonishing. At just 5 percent turnover, an active strategy would have to produce 100 basis points (or 1 percent) of additional gain to equal a passive return of 15 percent with no turnover—not an easy task. And the negative impact of increased turnover on after-tax returns is felt most keenly as turnover commences. For example, if portfolio turnover were increased from 20 percent to 25 percent, 75 basis points of additional alpha would be required to equalize the returns on an after-tax basis. But a 5 percent increase in turnover at the higher end of the range—from 80 percent

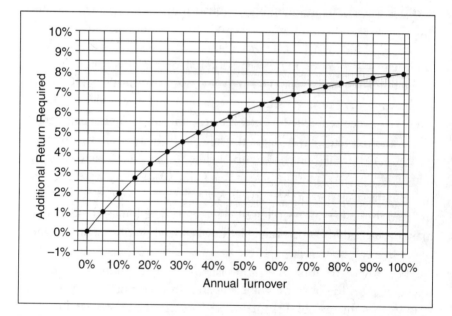

Figure 9.1   **Amount of Alpha Generation Required to Achieve 15 Percent per Annum after Taxes**

As portfolio turnover increases, the amount of additional return required to equal the market return also increases. Most active managers turn their portfolios 75–100 percent per annum. Passively managed stock index funds have an average annual turnover of about 5 percent.

to 85 percent, for example—requires additional alpha generation of just 17 basis points. Therefore, investors are cautioned to be especially attentive about turnover increases at the lower end of the spectrum.

Unfortunately, most clients who utilize active portfolio managers are subject to a much higher degree of portfolio turnover than the foregoing examples described. Many active managers boast a portfolio turnover rate of 100 percent—meaning that at the end of any given year, the holdings of the investor's portfolio are completely different than they were at the beginning of the year. A strategy that produces such rapid turnover would have to generate a staggering 800 basis points of excess return to equal the market return. It should also be noted that this analysis does not consider the effects of transaction costs on return, which would likely increase the alpha generation requirement above 10 percent per annum—a nearly impossible hurdle, even for the most talented of active managers.

From this analysis, it seems clear that managing a taxable portfolio is an entirely different task from managing one that is not subject to taxation (pension plans, individual retirement accounts, and 401(k) assets fall into this nontaxed category). Active portfolio managers would do well to examine their alpha generation and turnover on a historical basis and to make adjustments for taxable clients to the extent that their excess returns do not cover the tax consequences. It is quite possible that alpha-producing strategies that are prudent for tax-exempt clientele are not suited for those more sensitive to the realization of capital gains.

$$\alpha$$

Now that the effects of taxes have been examined from the perspective of the investment professional, it is time to consider the situation from the investor's point of view. A major consideration for any taxable investor should be the minimization of realized capital gains. This is certainly not rocket science; in fact, the relationship between unrealized gains, realized gains, and total return can be expressed as follows:

$$\text{Total Return} = \text{Realized Gains} + \text{Unrealized Gains}$$

Thus, at a given level of return, if one is minimizing realized gains, they must also be maximizing unrealized gains. Using the example from above, a $1,000 investment held for 10 years at a 15 percent average annual return would be worth approximately $4,045 assuming no portfolio turnover. In this case, unrealized gains would equal the difference between the original cost basis of the investment ($1,000) and the current value of the investment ($4,045), or $3,045. And because there was no portfolio turnover, no gains were realized, and hence no taxes are owed.

As portfolio turnover is introduced, the illustration becomes a bit more complex (Figure 9.2). At 10 percent portfolio turnover, for example, realized gains would equal 10 percent of the total return, or $15 on the

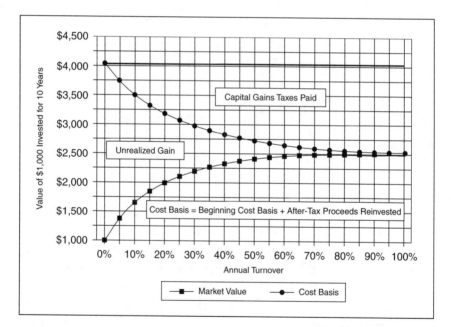

Figure 9.2   Portfolio Turnover, Taxes, and Return (15 Percent Average Return for 10 Years)

At any given level of return, a profit-maximizing investor should attempt to maximize his or her unrealized capital gains, which also minimizes both the capital gains taxes and the cost basis of the portfolio.

$1,000 investment. From the foregoing equation, the unrealized gain must therefore be $135 ($150 total return minus the realized gain of $15). Taxed at a 35 percent rate, the realized gain of $15 is now worth $9.75. Since this portion is now in cash and must be reinvested, the cost basis is now $1,009.75. The cost basis will rise every year, as long as cash is generated from the sale of securities in the portfolio (i.e., as long as portfolio turnover is greater than zero).

Thus, at any given level of return, after-tax profits are maximized when both the cost basis and capital gains taxes are *minimized*. This is, of course, at the same point at which unrealized gains are *maximized*—when portfolio turnover is zero. Although zero turnover, which represents a totally static portfolio, is nearly impossible to achieve, a number of strategies can be used to preserve a taxable investor's valuable stash of unrealized gains.

The first and most obvious solution is to utilize passive indexing. To generate alpha for their taxable clients, active money managers must clear three hurdles—fees, transaction costs, and the taxes that result from portfolio turnover. For this reason, actively managed strategies should always be benchmarked against the after-taxed performance of an indexed alternative. A well-known study in the *Journal of Portfolio Management* found that only two stock mutual funds out of 71 managed to beat the after-tax return of their respective indices between 1982 and 1991 by a significant margin.[3]

Many proponents of active management would disagree with this analysis, because it does not consider the possibility that a portfolio manager could foresee the beginning of a bear market. In this scenario, the manager could exit the client's positions and avoid the resulting decline in the markets. Dodging a significant drop in the stock market, they argue, would more than compensate for a spate of fees, commissions, and capital gains taxes.

But there is an alternative to blithely liquidating a portfolio when markets appear to be heading for trouble. In this case, the utilization of the futures markets is a much more appealing strategy for a taxable investor. Instead of selling the entire portfolio, initiating a short position of an appropriate amount in the stock index futures market would equivalently "hedge" the client against adverse market conditions while preserving the unrealized capital gains from the clutches of the Internal Revenue Service (IRS). And since marketable securities can be posted as margin for trading futures, the investor's stock positions would be unaffected by the transaction. This strategy is often referred to as an *overlay*, because the introduction of futures does not require the liquidation of the underlying securities. Although not universally accepted, overlay strategies have gained popularity among large institutional investors and sophisticated high net-worth individuals.

α

Considering the previous discussion, a portfolio that is designed to be both tax efficient and capable of earning excess return should be divvied into two piles. The first (and largest) pile should be those holdings that passively mimic a broad index like the Standard & Poor's (S&P) 500 or the Lehman Brothers Corporate/Government Bond Index. The second pile, which is directed by active management, should be those investments that add value through the use of other markets or strategies. To qualify for inclusion into the active portion of the portfolio, an advisor must be able to either produce return in excess of the after-tax return of his given benchmark, or to add diversification with an acceptable ratio of return-to-risk. The returns generated from the second pile should enable the portfolio to exceed the returns of the passive indices, while reducing risk. Note that the overlay strategy discussed previously is a variant of this portfolio. But because the overlay requires only minimal funding overlay, nearly all of the cash can be invested in the passive portion of the portfolio. Thus, the passive-active overlay portfolio may be capable of producing a higher return than a passive-active portfolio that does not utilize an overlay.

Finally, the fees paid to investment managers should vary between piles. The passive managers should be compensated nominally, since the mechanistic fashion in which they invest (i.e., buying all of the stocks in the S&P 500 index and holding them forever) is easily reproducible. The active managers, however, should be paid based on returns that are generated in excess of a given benchmark.

α

Thus far, we have discussed several ways to minimize the tax burden for investors. The third strategy, very simply, is *tax avoidance*. Starting with the early tax assessments during the times of the Egyptian Pharaohs, opposition to taxation has been the norm in most societies. This is certainly true for the United States, where taxation was indelibly linked to early colonial commerce. The first instance of widespread tax evasion in the New World occurred when the English Parliament passed the Navigation Act of 1651. The ordinance required that all goods originating from the colonies be transported by English ships, which allowed duties to be collected when these goods were traded between countries.[4] Colonial businessmen were quick to realize that bartering such goods with Dutch merchants not only yielded higher prices, but also loosened the grip of London's Puritan merchants on colonial trade. As a result, the colonists ignored the law.

Keeping with the spirit of American patriotism, tax shelters—which either avoid or defer taxation—have been an American institution since the passage of the first income tax in 1862 (which less than 1 percent of the population bothered to pay). Most tax shelters were eliminated in the 1986 Tax Reform Act, especially those involving real estate investments. But that only reinvigorated the creative abilities of individuals intent on avoiding one of the more inevitable costs of life.

For instance, many Wall Street firms have developed ways for their clients to avoid realizing short-term gains (which are taxed at a 39.6 percent rate) by converting them into long-term gains (which are taxed at an 18–20 percent rate). The typical arrangement involves a wealthy investor interested in a hedge fund or other actively managed investment. But instead of the investor directly putting money into the fund, a swap contract is entered with a securities firm. The firm promises to match the fund's return, but the investor is not paid anything until after the 18-month period for long-term gains has passed.

The hybrid contract between the investor and the firm gains (or loses) value in line with the fund's reported results. But since it is a contract and not a direct investment in the fund, the investor is not liable for any short-term gains he does not receive. The investor thus not only gets a lower tax rate, but may also defer paying taxes until the contract expires. Securities firms charge a fee of 1 or 2 percent of the dollar amount covered by such a contract—a lot less than the tax differential, assuming the fund racks up acceptable returns.[5]

Critics of tax shelters claim that such schemes hurt the economy by wasting the resources of lawyers and accountants who design these complicated but economically meaningless arrangements. At worst, they redirect investment capital from uses that make economic sense. For instance, in the early 1980s the tax system made it profitable to build office buildings even if there were no tenants to occupy them. The result was downtown areas filled with "see through" towers and a real estate glut from which some cities are still recovering.[6]

Many tax experts warn that such swaps may be an endangered species because Congress will soon be searching for revenue-raising measures to help pay for tax cuts incurred in recent legislation.[7] But it is doubtful that any new law would be retroactive. Even if swaps are disallowed, other tax dodging strategies are likely to pop up. One idea would be to route the income through a foreign entity (or a domestic tax-exempt entity) that is not subject to U.S. taxes.[9]

In short, effective tax shelters should be both cost-effective and immune from legislation. If such a structure existed, many people would be attracted to it, which would likely increase the attention paid to it by the IRS. Thus, it is probably more profitable in the long run to focus one's energy on creating better portfolios by creating a more tax-efficient mousetrap.

Chapter 10

Behavioral Finance: Are We Really That Irrational?

> There is an impressive and growing body of evidence demonstrating that investors and speculators don't necessarily learn from experience. Emotion overrides logic time after time.
>
> *David Dreman*
> *Chairman, Dreman Value Advisors*

What drives investor behavior? Much financial theory is based on the notion that everyone acts rationally—attempting to maximize their gain and minimize their pain—when making investment decisions. Modern portfolio theory, for example, assumes that investors seek to earn the highest return at any given level of risk. The arbitrage pricing theory posits that two identical securities cannot sell at different prices for very long, because rationally minded traders will buy the cheap and sell the dear until both are priced identically. And the efficient market hypothesis preaches the futility of using new information to generate excess return, because the universe of rational investors will act in such a way that the information is instantaneously reflected in asset prices. In the world of the totally rational investor, the best one can hope for is the return of the stock market—minus commissions, management fees, and taxes.

Rational behavior is one of the most accepted assumptions in social science. Not only is rationality intuitively appealing, but the ease with which it can be mathematically modeled greatly simplifies research. For these reasons, rationality is well accepted by economists and plays a fundamental role in their interpretation of economic behavior.

Despite its obvious attractiveness, it has long been known that utility theory systematically mispredicts human behavior. The reason for this apparent lack of sensible thought most likely derives from the inner workings of the human brain. If a computer is asked to choose between two alternatives, it will calculate potential gains or losses by their respective probabilities in making its choice. Humans, with their limited cognitive abilities, will most likely make a judgment call based on a number of learned principles that do not require the computational capabilities inherent in many machines. These principles, or rules of thumb, make for the most efficient use of our capacity to factor insight and reasoning into the decision-making process. But since rules of thumb are merely approximations of reality, their use often creates bias and error. Rational choice theory is thus an excellent guide to how decision *should be* made, but it does not reflect how decisions *are* made.[1]

Consider the well-known predilection of individuals to be more afraid of a loss than desirous of a gain—a tendency that can lead to some quite irrational decisions. Research has shown that losing one dollar makes the average investor feel twice as bad as winning one dollar makes them feel good. As a result, investors are much more likely to hold on to sinking stocks and sell stocks that are appreciating in value. This one bias—frequently referred to as *regret theory*—could explain the inability of some individual investors to profit even in bull markets. In his humorous book *Winner Take All*, William Gallacher takes aim at the human propensity for loss avoidance:

> Could there be a way to harness the power of the chronic "steady state" loser? Theoretically, yes. Imagine we form a trading team from among the most consistently bad traders we know. Now we ask this team to trade for the sole objective of losing money. Will these chronic losers now be able to lose when they want to, in the same way they lost when they were trying to win?

Not a chance. They will win, simply because they are trying to lose. The reason for this apparent paradox is that, while the chronic loser's *objective* may be changed, his *behavior* in pursuit of that objective cannot be changed. Faced with the bizarre objective of trying to lose, the chronic loser will grab at losses quickly because taking losses will be instantly gratifying. Likewise, he will avoid taking profits on winners, since all his instincts will tell him to procrastinate.[2]

Regret theory is also helpful in explaining another human frailty—herding. Many people find it easy to buy a popular stock, because if it depreciates there are other investors who are faced with similar losses. Thus, acting counter to conventional wisdom is difficult because it raises the possibility of feeling regret if such actions prove incorrect. Unfortunately, even professional investors are not immune from this bias. Studies have shown that investment advisors tend to buy stock in well-known and popular companies because they are less likely to be fired if they underperform. Stock analysts engage in herd behavior in part because they are constantly evaluated against their peers, though research suggests that when forecasting earnings, young analysts tend to try to fit in with the crowd—even if the crowd is wrong—more than more seasoned ones.[3] When analysts are older and more established, it is possible that they face less risk in pursuing an independent line of thought, but an analyst's report that is radically different is a rare occurrence on Wall Street.

Related to regret theory is the human tendency to place particular emphasis on the most recently available information. As a result, investors have a penchant to become overly optimistic when the market goes up and exceedingly pessimistic when the market goes down, which may explain why stock prices often rise dramatically on good news and drop sharply on bad news.

In his 1938 book *The General Theory of Employment, Interest, and Money*, John Maynard Keynes frequently discusses the importance of psychological factors in investing. He coined the term *animal spirits* to describe "the spontaneous urge to action" frequently exhibited in manias and market crashes. According to Keynes:

> We should not conclude from this that everything depends on waves of irrational psychology. On the contrary, the state of long-term expectation is often steady, and, when it is not, the other factors exert their compensating effects. We are merely reminding ourselves that human decisions affecting the future, whether personal or political or economic, cannot depend on strict mathematical expectation, since the basis for making such calculations does not exist; and that it is our innate urge to activity which makes the wheels go round, our rational selves choosing between the alternatives as best as we are able, calculating where we can, but often falling back from our motive on whim or sentiment or chance.[4]

As Wall Street and academia have come to realize the limits of their financial models and algorithms, behavioral finance has become an increasingly popular area for research. This could be due, in part, to the realization that financial engineering and other complex mathematical methodologies can reveal some, but not all, of the characteristics of markets. The behavioral approach is an attempt not to understand just the nuances of financial instruments, but also the mysteries of the human beings that buy and sell them. Bond analysts can sympathize with this view. Mortgage-backed securities traders have numerous mathematical pricing models by which they value even the most exotic derivative products. Nonetheless, mortgage-related hedge funds continue to implode because no one has yet determined how quickly different types of homeowners will refinance their mortgages when interest rates change.[5] If quantitative analysis alone can not solve the problem, perhaps the study of human behavior can shed light in a darkened crevice.

One of the most prominent proponents of behavioral finance is Andrew Lo at the Massachusetts Institute of Technology, who successfully poked enough holes in the efficient market hypothesis 10 years ago (at the age of 28) to make him a leading authority in quantitative finance. Lo often mentions "a general malaise" when describing recent studies in capital markets, a view also shared by Merton Miller, the 1990 winner of the Nobel prize in economics. Lo's new focus on behavioral finance involves determining how biological changes affect decision making. He plans to hook up groups of traders and nontraders to magnetic resonance imaging devices to determine what regions of the brain are most engaged when individuals focus on risky decisions. Lo hopes to narrow down the possible genes that could play a role in making someone a natural-born risk-taker or trader. The project is an audacious and risky venture. Scientists have yet to finish mapping the human genome, and the analytical tools necessary to pinpoint something as hypothetical as a risk gene may not be available for years.[6]

In less than two decades, the study of behavioral finance has progressed from academic theory to real-world application. Some of the brightest minds in finance have embraced its implicit logic to explain the baffling volatility of financial markets. In their 1985 paper "Does the Stock Market Overreact?," Richard Thaler and Werner DeBondt tested whether extreme movements of stock prices in one direction are subsequently followed by extreme movements in the other direction. They studied more than one thousand stocks over a period of 60 years, and classified the stocks that had gone up by more (or had fallen by less) than the market average in each 3-year period as winners. The stocks that had gone up by less (or had fallen by more) than the market average were classified losers. They then calculated the average performance of each group over the subsequent 3 years. Their results showed that portfolios of losing stocks outperformed those of winning stocks by a wide margin.

Thaler and DeBondt believe that the tendency of stocks to fall in and out of favor is the result of the human tendency to overweight recent evidence and to lose sight of the long run. A common interpretation of this result is that when there is a sustained streak of good news about a stock, its price overshoots its fundamental value and must ultimately experience a correction. Similarly, a preponderance of bad news can send the price of a stock far below its intrinsic value, so that in the long run an extended rally should ensue when the fortunes of the company finally reverse.

Buoyed by the findings of his study, Thaler went on to write *The Winner's Curse* in 1992, a book that describes a number of paradoxes that exist in the realm of finance. Among other economic irregularities, Thaler details the human tendency to bid too aggressively in an auction as the number of competing bidders increases and why gamblers go for long shots at the end of a losing day. Ultimately, he urges his colleagues to take a more balanced view of economics—one that considers both the rationality assumptions of his predecessors and the often enigmatic biases of human nature.

Three years later, Thaler was offered an endowed chair at the center of the efficient market universe, the University of Chicago. It was a turning point for both him and behavioral finance. Students who came to learn hard-core finance could also sign up for Thaler's elective course, called Managerial Decision Making, which is described as a class "only recommended for those who expect to have to make decisions during their careers." Thaler begins the class with a variant of a famous behavioral study that found that 90 percent of Swedish drivers consider themselves better than average—a mathematical impossibility. Similarly, Thaler asks his students where they think they will rank in the course's final grading. Of the 125 MBAs taking the course, not a single student thought they would finish in the bottom half. "Obviously, half of them were wrong," cracks Thaler.[7]

But Thaler does not restrict his usage of behavioral finance to parlor tricks for his graduate students. Along with Russell Fuller (the former chairman of the finance department at Washington State University), he is a partner at Fuller and Thaler Asset Management in San Mateo, California. Like many behavioral-based asset managers, Fuller and Thaler are primarily value investors. Their use of the value approach emanates from their belief that a contrarian strategy that emphasizes companies that are out of favor with Wall Street analysts will over time earn a superior risk-adjusted return.

Behaviorists were not the first to espouse the value approach to investing. In *Security Analysis*, Benjamin Graham expressed disdain for Wall Street's near obsession with earnings in determining the value of a stock. Although the book was written in 1933, Graham's observation that investors pay too much for trendy stocks and too little for companies that are out of favor strikes a familiar chord with many modern-day market pundits. But the reasons the two camps are attracted to the value approach are entirely different.

Many proponents of value investing believe that such stocks outperform simply because they are riskier than growth stocks. Since value stocks are those issues that have the lowest price-earnings ratios, the lowest capitalizations, and the highest dividend yields, these stocks are likely more vulnerable in an economic downturn than more established growth stocks. Thus, investors would have to realize a higher return to justify the additional risk in owning them. If this is the case, the so-called value premium is not an anomaly, but the well-documented tendency of riskier investments to earn a higher return than their less-risky counterparts—the central tenet of Markowitz's modern portfolio theory.

Counter to the value premium explanation, behaviorists reference their belief in a "value characteristic." In essence, the value characteristic is the tendency of investors to prefer a growth stock (i.e., a strong, solid company) to a value stock (a distressed company). For behaviorists, risk is not the driving force behind the difference in return; it is much more a function of investor preferences. And since the difference in return is not due to risk, the value premium is considered by behaviorists to be a deviation from the efficient market hypothesis.

Of course, there are still plenty of academics and practitioners who are skeptical about the existence of the value premium. Some have argued that the effect is a chance result that is unlikely to be observed out of sample. Others indicate that the value effect works almost exclusively with small-cap stocks and is only robust enough to be detected during the month of January, when individuals do the most tax-loss selling.

Of course, there are many willing critics of both modern portfolio theory and the capital asset pricing model. Milton Friedman provided the definitive response to such criticisms when he argued that theories should not be evaluated on the basis of their assumptions, but rather on their predictive power. An expert billiards player, for instance, may not know the laws of physics, but he will act as if he knows such laws. In this setting, both the efficient market hypothesis and modern portfolio theory have successfully explained most market behavior observed since Louis Bachelier's landmark study of security prices in 1900.

α

Proponents of the behavioral approach do not limit themselves to capturing the tendency for stocks to change direction—going from winners to losers and vice versa—in the long run. Behaviorists also cite the tendency of stock prices (and the price of other assets) to exhibit trending behavior in the short run.

Stocks have also been shown to trend after the release of public information (Figure 10.1). Examples of the types of information that can cause this effect include earnings announcements, stock issues and repurchases, dividend initiations and omissions, and analyst recommendations.[8]

The existence of trends could be consistent with the traditional models of price behavior (i.e., the market efficiency), to the extent that they

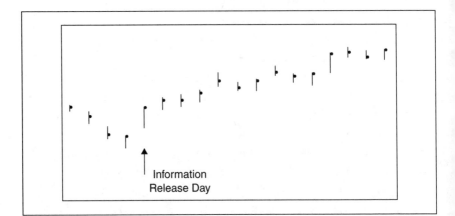

Figure 10.1   **Trend after Information Release**
Stocks have been found to trend following announcements of earnings and other company-specific information. The trending behavior is short-lived, however, and is frequently followed by a sharp reversal.

reflect variations in risk. But unlike pure value strategies, where there is a division over the role of risk in the profitability of value strategies, there seems to be more of a consensus that short-horizon price trends are not inextricably linked to enhanced risk. Several studies have rejected risk as an explanation for postearnings announcement drift.[9] Eugene Fama has remarked that short-term momentum is the "main embarrassment" to the risk explanation.[10]

An intriguing explanation for trending price behavior has been developed by Harrison Hong at Stanford Business School and Jeremy Stein at the Massachusetts Institute of Technology Sloan School of Management.[11] The two researchers modeled a market populated by two groups of short-term traders—newswatchers and momentum traders. Neither type of trader is rational in the traditional sense (i.e., able to interpret all available information about a stock instantaneously). Rather, they are boundedly rational in that they are able to process only a certain subset of information. The newswatchers make forecasts based on publicly available fundamental information such as earnings and corporate cash flow; their limitation is that they do not consider past price changes. Conversely, momentum traders do condition on past price changes, but they do not consider company fundamentals.

According to Hong and Stein's behavioral model, when only newswatchers are active, stock prices adjust slowly to releases of information. There are several reasons for this characteristic, but the demon that most plagues the newswatchers is a bias called the *disjunction effect*. This is the tendency of individuals to defer a decision in the face of uncertainty. In making a choice, subjects have been observed to wait until additional information is revealed, even if that information is not needed in making the decision.[12]

The researchers then added the momentum traders to the mix. Since these traders only consider price action in their decision making, they observe the trending behavior caused by the newswatcher's activities. The momentum players then buy the stocks that were purchased by the newswatchers, thus accelerating the stock's upward price direction. Eventually, prices exceed the stock's fundamental value to the extent that a dose of bad news causes a dramatic overreaction, and the price of the stock drops dramatically.

Hong and Stein (along with Terrence Lim from the Amos Tuck School at Dartmouth College) followed their research with another study 10 months later. Their intent was to determine if a stock's market capitalization (the aggregate value of a firm's outstanding stock) was related to the tendency of information to be only slowly (and not instantaneously) reflected in stock prices. It seems plausible that news about small-cap stocks gets out more slowly. This might be observed, for example, if investors face fixed costs for the acquisition of information and choose to devote more effort to learning about those stocks in which they can take larger positions.

The study also investigated whether stocks that receive a relatively low amount of coverage from Wall Street analysts react to information more slowly than those stocks that are more closely followed. But since analyst coverage is closely related to firm size, the researchers made adjustments in their study to control for the dependence of these two variables.

Hong, Stein, and Lim obtained the predicted results for both firm size and analyst coverage. With respect to size, as one moves past the very smallest small-cap stocks, the profitability of momentum strategies declines sharply. And as one holds firm size fixed, momentum strategies work particularly well among stocks that have low analyst coverage. Beyond being statistically significant, the effects were also of an economically interesting magnitude. Across the entire sample, momentum profits were roughly 60 percent greater among the one-third of the stocks with the lowest amount of coverage, as compared to the one-third with the highest amount of coverage.[13]

The study also revealed another interesting abnormality. Low-coverage stocks seem to react more sluggishly to bad news than to good news. But this may have more to do with manager behavior than market behavior. For example, suppose a firm with no analyst coverage has just released positive information on its prospects. To the extent that its managers prefer higher to lower stock prices, they will take extra effort to ensure that as many potential investors as possible receive the news. Conversely, if the same firm is sitting on bad news, its managers will have much less incentive to bring investors up to date. Thus, the marginal contribution of outside analysts in getting the news out is likely to be greater when the news is bad.

$$\alpha$$

Although it is interesting to observe the behavioral tendency of individual stocks, the circumstances that lead to a collective group mindset are far more engrossing. Such was the case during the chaotic market environment of the early 1970s. In those days, the Nifty Fifty stocks were all the rage. These stocks—the largest of the large-capitalization issues listed on the New York Stock Exchange—were trading at valuation levels unheard of for stocks at that time. Banks, corporate trust departments, and investment firms, reluctant to miss out on the opportunity, bought these stocks with reckless abandon for fear that they would be left out of the party. The scenario closely paralleled an even more perplexing economic period three hundred years earlier commonly referred to as "Tulipomania."

Tulips were first imported from Turkey to Europe in the late sixteenth century, where they rapidly caught the fancy of wealthy noblemen, especially those of Dutch descent. By 1634, the tulip's popularity increased to the point that "it was deemed a proof of bad taste in any man of fortune to be without a collection of them."[14] Curiously, the inferior nature of the tulip, particularly compared to that of a rose (which is easier to cultivate, more colorful, and considerably more fragrant) was never a hindrance to its value. The demand for tulips increased so much that by 1636, bulbs were traded on the Amsterdam Stock Exchange. Many wealthy families were known to have spent their entire fortunes for a handful of roots, only to sell them later for even more money. The height of the mania brought about some unusual circumstances, particularly among those who were not aware of the plant's perceived value. Several recorded instances of individuals confusing tulip bulbs with onions have been substantiated, making for the world's most expensive meal at the time (the unfortunate gourmands were forced to spend time in prison until the debt could be repaid).

The Nifty Fifty stocks in the 1970s never reached the pinnacle of the tulip three centuries prior, but their rise was nonetheless stunning. Eastman Kodak was the group's star performer and an excellent example of the period's euphoria for high-cap stocks. In 1972, Kodak's sales were $3.5 billion and it was valued in the market at $24 billion—the same as General Motors, which at the time had sales of more than $30 billion.[15] Investment professionals who were not overweighed in the Nifty Fifty lagged their competitors by a wide margin, since the stocks of other well-known industrial concerns failed to reach new highs during the market advance. The popularity of the high caps created what was commonly referred to as the "two-tiered" market: As the price/earnings (P/E) ratio of the Nifty Fifty averaged around 30, their counterparts in the Standard & Poor's (S&P) 500 sported an average P/E of 11—the lowest level since 1957.[16] How had the U.S. stock market, a model of efficient price discovery, become so bipolar? The answer lies in the competitive nature of the investment business.

Much like today, money management firms in the early 1970s enjoyed economies of scale that allowed for increases in client assets with minimal increases in fixed costs. As a result, firms vigorously competed for the accounts of pension funds, endowments, and wealthy individuals. The largest investment advisors at the time were two banks, Morgan Guaranty ($16.6 billion in employee-benefit assets at the end of 1972) and Banker's Trust ($15 billion).[17] Since both firms had a reputation for investing in growth stocks, their performance for the 10 years ending in 1972 was significantly better than those advisors who used a more diversified methodology to manage client assets. The pressure placed on newer advisors to meet or exceed the returns of these two behemoths was substantial—so much so that many of these smaller firms started mimicking the bank's portfolios. Of the 17 banks polled by *Forbes* in 1972, 14 listed IBM, then the markets' biggest stock, as their top holding (the other 3 had it in second place); and some had as much as 13 percent of their client's assets in that one stock![18] Crowd psychology had replaced common sense.

It was said that "the force of example brought the flowers into great favor, and amongst a certain class of people tulips have ever since been prized more highly than any other flower on the earth."[19] If the fancy of

Dutch aristocracy caused the tulip to increase in value, it was the economic law of supply and demand that perpetuated its demise. Although the speculative bubble in Holland only lasted for a few years, enough damage was done to impair the country's economy for 50 years. Wealthy families were nearly reduced to beggary; many that had emerged from the dregs of society were cast back into their original obscurity. Any persons left with tulip bulbs, which had decreased in price by approximately 90 percent, might have certainly made relish from the "onions."

The parallel in the Nifty Fifty stocks, although not as dramatic or economically devastating as Tulipomania, still underscores the end result of crowd behavior. Just four years later, with the market at about the same level as 1972, Kodak was down 20 percent, with other high-cap issues down nearly four times that amount. Meanwhile, the stocks of long-ignored, solid companies like U.S. Steel more than doubled. M. S. Forbes said of the period: "Obviously the problem was not with the companies but with the temporary insanity of institutional money managers—proving again that stupidity well-packaged can sound like wisdom."[20]

In the present day, many observers have noted the extreme furor over Internet stocks. At the end of 1998, the market valuation of Charles Schwab, a discount broker with on-line trading facilities, surpassed that of Merrill Lynch. eBay, a recently founded on-line auction house, outstripped Sotheby's. America Online (AOL), an Internet service provider, became more valuable than the Disney Corporation. One analyst described the stock of Amazon.com, which rose 1,800 percent in 1998, as "the most outrageously priced equity in the world," but advised buying the stock nonetheless.[21] In *The Road Ahead*, Microsoft CEO Bill Gates describes the frenzy as a gold rush, commenting that "a few [investments] will pay off, but when the frenzy is behind us, we will look back incredulously at the wreckage of failed ventures and wonder, 'Who funded those companies? What was going on in their minds? Was that just mania at work?'"[22]

$$\alpha$$

Ted Aronson, the head of the highly respected investment firm Aronson and Partners, has often been quoted as saying that investing in an actively managed fund is an act of faith. "Under normal circumstance," he says, "it takes between 20 and 800 years of monitoring performance to statistically prove that a money manager is skillful rather than lucky—which is a lot more than most people have in mind when they say 'long term.'" [23] Similarly, the arguments expounded by behaviorists have not been universally accepted as the ultimate explanation for asset returns. The field is still relatively young, and a great amount of research needs to be done. Of course, by that time it is likely that markets will have adapted to such revelations, making it even more difficult to exploit the market's behavioral tendencies.

Chapter 11

Technology and
the Capital Markets

There can be few fields of human endeavor in which history
counts for so little as in the world of finance.

John Kenneth Galbraith

The business of U.S. oil production was changed single-handedly by a
one-armed mechanic from southern Texas named Patillo Higgins. The
year was 1889, and Higgins became interested in a hill that rose above the
flat coastal plain near Beaumont after taking his Baptist Sunday school
class there for a picnic. Higgins had discovered half a dozen small bubbling
springs, and lit the gas that escaped from them. The children were quite
amused; Higgins was intrigued. The hill was called Spindletop, and Higgins became convinced that an abundance of cheap oil lay beneath it.[1]

Higgins commenced drilling in 1893. He met with no success at this
first attempt. Later efforts in 1895 and 1896 also failed to find oil. Although Higgins had promised his partners that they would become rich,
they began to lose faith in the project. Higgins became jokingly referred to
as "The Millionaire."

In spite of his difficulties, Higgins never lost faith in his vision. He
eventually convinced a mining engineer named Anthony Lucas, who had
considerable experience prospecting in salt domes like Spindletop, of the
potential of the region. Lucas felt that the area could yield a well with a
production of 50 barrels per day. They hired Guffy and Galey, the most

famous and successful wildcatting team of that era and commenced operations in the fall of 1900. On January 10, 1901, while attempting to free their drill from a rock formation, the famous Lucas Gusher blew. Oil sprayed more than a hundred feet above the derrick for nine days until the well was capped. The actual production of the well was an astounding 80,000 barrels per day. It was the beginning of the Texas oil boom.

Higgins's experience is similar in many ways to that of Richard Olsen, who assembled a team of physicists and statisticians to study tick-by-tick data from financial markets. Conventional wisdom held that trading information of that detail was useless noise. But in the last few years, economic orthodoxy has embraced Olsen's view. "Academics as well as traders recognize that potentially lucrative information is embedded in the seemingly chaotic movements of prices from moment to moment," according to a 1997 article in Business Week.[2] Market microstructure is now one of the most active research areas in finance.

But like oil reserves, which naturally decline as oil fields are drained, market inefficiencies dry up as more traders enter the fray. Just one year after Higgins's discovery, there were 285 active wells operating at Spindletop. Similarly, there are more active investment management firms than ever before. Participants in both of these businesses have realized that with increased competition, developing a strategic advantage is of paramount importance.

Both the oil industry and the investment management business have embraced technology to develop an edge in the marketplace. Computer power has roughly doubled every 18 months—a prediction made in 1974 by Intel founder Gordon Moore that has been amazingly accurate. Instead of relying on gut instinct like Mr. Higgins, petroleum conglomerates are now using three-dimensional seismic imaging and microbial soil analysis to determine where hidden caches of oil may lie. The high cost of these new tools and the steadily declining amount of oil left to be found have made the oil business quite competitive. As a result, only the most highly capitalized firms have been able to maintain exploration facilities.

David Shaw, a former computer science professor cum investment manager, stated that when his firm was founded in the early 1980s, a number of easily identifiable market inefficiencies could be exploited. The profits earned from this trading could be used to subsidize the costly research required to find more esoteric market eccentricities. According to Shaw, increased competition has caused many strategies that used to work to disappear. He has stated that his firm has spent hundreds of millions of dollars in research.[3] There is no question that technology plays an important role in investment management, but an overreliance on computers in the development of a sustainable advantage can introduce several problems.

The first is the danger of "curvefitting." Computers may unleash new investment opportunities, but sometimes they foster the illusion that a false methodology has merit. If enough trading rules are considered over time, some rules are bound by pure luck to produce superior performance, even if they do not genuinely possess predictive power over asset returns. For instance, David Leinweber, managing director of First Quadrant Associates L.P., sifted through a United Nations database and found that the single best predictor of the Standard & Poor's (S&P) 500 stock index was butter production in Bangladesh.[4] But most of the time, distinguishing between a statistical anomaly and a tradable inefficiency is not as easy as the foregoing example would indicate.

To make matters worse, many psychologists believe that the human brain has a strong tendency to make errors in judgment. One of the most persistent areas of illusion is a tendency toward overconfidence. Many studies have shown that, when asked questions that require considerable reasoning to solve, the level of accuracy increases with the respondent's intelligence. But the degree of confidence in the validity of those answers increases to a much greater degree. Overconfidence is at its greatest in our own area of expertise—just when it can do the most damage. Cognitive illusions, according to researchers Amos Tversky and Daniel Kahneman, are "neither rational nor capricious."[5]

Another frequently encountered perceptual flaw is known as *anchoring*. A classic experiment consists of asking a subject the percentage of African nations there are in the United Nations. Before asking the question, the researcher turns a wheel of fortune in full view of the subject, stopping it on some number between 1 and 100. The researcher frequently tells the subject that the number of the wheel has absolutely no relation to the question, but invariably the number has a strong effect on the answer given by the respondent. If the number 12 comes up, for example, the answer is likely to be smaller than if the wheel stops on 90.[6] The subjects unconsciously anchored their responses to the randomly selected number.

Propagandists frequently use anchoring in altering societal opinion. During the Gulf War, the Bush administration followed bulletins of allied air attacks with extremely low estimates of civilian Iraqi casualties (their announcement varied from 2 to 10 deaths per incident). Their intent was to prevent public opinion from swaying away from President Bush's imperative against Saddam Hussein. Pentagon officials were betting that even the most skeptical observers would anchor their mental adjustments close to the original "estimate."[7] Only after hostilities ended did the real figures surface (actual numbers were in the tens of thousands), but by then public opinion was of little consequence.

Anchoring and curvefitting often go hand in hand. Because securities price changes have a tendency to exhibit more extreme outliers than one would expect, traditional statistical techniques are often not usable in market analysis. The remaining nonparametric statistical tools are much more inferential in nature—meaning that the results must be interpreted. If the results of such a study are in conflict with the analyst's first impressions, she may struggle to overcome her original hypothesis. She may (either consciously or unconsciously) incorporate as many constraints in her research as possible to prove her first impression. In this case, anchoring is given full backing by pride and self-satisfaction.

An overreliance on technology also fosters a mistaken belief that a commitment to employing the most powerful computers will give one a distinct advantage over one's competitors. In reality, such a commitment only reduces the possibility that one is not left behind by the competition. The profits associated with money management are sufficiently high that an investment firm's search for a performance edge is rarely constrained by a lack of technology. As a result, nearly all investment managers have proportionately large research and development budgets. And when a number of these firms begin to operate in the same markets with similar strategies, the degree of market efficiency can rise dramatically.

Andrew Lo and A. Craig Mackinlay put a unique spin on this issue in their book *A Non-Random Walk Down Wall Street*. When they began examining stock price changes in 1985, they were shocked to find a substantial degree of autocorrelative behavior—evidence that previous price changes could have been used to forecast changes in the next period. Their findings were sufficiently overwhelming as to refute the random walk hypothesis, which states that asset price changes are totally unpredictable.

The most important insight from their work occurred when they repeated the study 11 years later, using prices from 1986 to 1996. This newer data conformed more closely with the random walk model than the original sample period. Upon further investigation, they learned that over the past decade several investment firms—most notably Morgan Stanley and D. E. Shaw—were engaged in a type of stock trading specifically designed to take advantage of the kinds of patterns uncovered in their earlier study. Known at the time as *pairs trading*—and now referred to as *statistical arbitrage*—these strategies fared quite well until recently, but are now regarded as a very competitive and thin-margin business because of the proliferation of hedge funds engaged in this type of market activity.[8]

Lo and Mackinlay believe that the profits earned by the early statistical arbitrageurs can be viewed as economic "rents" that accrued via their innovation, creativity, and risk tolerance. Now that others have begun to reverse engineer and mimic their methodologies, profit margins are declining. Therefore, neither the evidence against the random walk, nor the more recent trend toward the random walk, are inconsistent with the practical version of the efficient market hypothesis.[9] In short, market inefficiencies are not always market opportunities.

$$\alpha$$

Due to the growing sophistication of market participants and increasing efficiency of markets, the investment management business has become a game in which success is measured by a painfully small margin of 1 to 2 percent per year. A combination of frustration and bafflement has led many money managers to place a higher priority on the numerous approaches to risk management than on the urgent search for maximum return. *Maybe I can't score a higher return than the competition, but perhaps I can make the same return with lower risk,* many seem to be thinking.

VaR (value at risk) is Wall Street's latest salvo in the attempt to quantify risk. Simply defined, VaR is an estimate of maximum potential loss to be expected over a chosen time frame. Its primary appeal is its ease of interpretation as a summary measure of risk, as well as its consistent treatment of risk across different financial instruments and asset classes. By describing risk using a possible percentage loss (i.e., "losses in the next month should not exceed 5 percent with 95 percent confidence") VaR facilitates direct comparisons of risk across different portfolios. But most importantly, the methodology boils risk down to one simple number, which can be quickly calculated and easily digested by senior management.

Financial innovation often follows a problem that has caused firms to lose substantial amounts of capital. VaR is no exception to this rule. The early 1990s were rife with one derivatives trading scandal after another. Daiwa Bank, NatWest, and Metallgesellschaft were but a few of the many financial companies, banks, and brokerages that were rocked by losses. But none were as big, or as shocking, as the losses experienced by Barings Bank, the venerable 233-year-old institution that proudly counted Queen Elizabeth as a client.

The incident occurred in the bank's Singapore office. The trader responsible for supervising the bank's Japanese stock-index arbitrage operation, Nick Leeson, apparently grew tired of the strategy's muted returns, and began making massive directional bets in the Nikkei stock index futures market. A working-class "barrow boy" who grew up in a rundown public housing project in London, Leeson stood to make a huge bonus if his bets were successful.

Unbeknownst to his superiors, Leeson was running a shell game, secretly hiding losses in a special ledger that he also controlled because Barings, in a cost-cutting move, allowed him to act as both trader and back-office settlement manager. Leeson kept up the charade for more than two years while earning more than $1 million annually in wages and bonuses.[10] Ultimately, the trading losses exceeded the capitalization of the company, and the oldest bank in London was purchased for £1 by Dutch ING Bank.

The Barings incident points to clear failures in the supervision of the company's activities by its senior management. Apparently, few of the bank's managers questioned the huge reported profits that were the result of a relatively low-risk arbitrage strategy. Simple common sense might have suggested that the reported results from Singapore were implausible. Yet, the bank continued pledging collateral for the operation until its demise.

Ironically, if Barings would have implemented a VaR system, it might not have prevented the collapse of the bank. Since VaR only monitors market risk, it cannot adequately reflect the risks associated with a liquidity crisis or with unsupervised personnel. The inability to capture many qualitative factors and exogenous risk variables points to the need to combine VaR with checks and balances, procedures, policies, controls, limits, and reserves.[11]

One of the positive attributes of VaR is its effect on bank compensation plans. The use of VaR has encouraged banks to evaluate their proprietary traders not only by the profit they make, but also by the risk that they are exposed to. Before value at risk, it was a common practice among banks to remunerate traders simply by their contribution to the banks' earnings, with no regard to potential losses. These traders might rationally believe that it is better for them to take extremely large risks to make a larger bonus, if the downside to such a gamble is merely the loss of employment. This type of personnel risk is commonly referred to as a *moral hazard*. Another example of a moral hazard is a driver who disregards a stoplight, knowing that if he crashes the insurance company will buy him a new vehicle.

$$\alpha$$

Despite its shortcomings, VaR is rapidly gaining acceptance in many large corporations. Indeed, if financial institutions are required to disclose their VaR risk profiles, regulators can more effectively calculate the capital adequacy an organization must hold in order to prevent default. VaR also enables firms to determine which businesses offer the greatest expected returns at the least level of risk. Considering the increasing acceptance of the VaR methodology, it is easy to understand why fiduciaries have tried to adopt the technology to the world of investment management. Unfortunately, the goals of risk management in banking and investing are quite different.

The first and foremost goal of risk management in banks is to avoid catastrophic losses. Banks must strive to give the appearance of being conservatively managed and insulated from financial shocks so that they can protect the bank's capital position and its core business, which is serving as a source of credit and liquidity in all market conditions.[12] Most banks operate their risk management units autonomously, which separates it from the various profit centers that it monitors.

In contrast to bankers, investment managers are charged with the responsibility of delivering performance above a stated benchmark. Further, alpha generation should be earned by taking reasonable risks, so that client accounts are not exposed to unnecessary peril during periods of market turmoil. It is not enough for investment managers to avoid large losses. They must constantly monitor the rate at which risk is taken and profits are accrued, even during normal market conditions. For this reason, the risk management function within an investment firm is usually fully integrated into the research and portfolio construction departments.

Bank risk managers are focused on the type of catastrophic risk that will compromise their asset base enough to force the bank out of business. There is little pressure on banks to increase their return on assets, which average slightly over one percent, because fees and commission income has become an increasingly large percentage of their revenues. Risk managers in the banking world are encouraged to use conservative risk estimates that are upwardly biased. The Bank of International Settlements, which formed a set of regulatory guidelines for banks in the Group of Ten countries, recommends multiplying potential market risks by a factor of three. Many banks follow this guideline. A risk manager in a bank will not get fired for overestimating risk.

For investment management, there is a serious cost to the overestimation of risk. If the risk level is incremented upward to be conservative, the ability of the manager to generate alpha is handicapped. By artificially constraining the amount of risk inherent in a portfolio, the threat of consistent underperformance is introduced.[13]

Investment managers who are considering utilizing a VaR system (or have been asked by a large client to do so) should pay attention to the method's sensitivity to changes in the variables used. Most of these variables are calculated using assumptions about the correlation between markets, the distribution of returns, and the amount of historical data used. A recent study examined eight common VaR methodologies and found that the results varied by more than 14 times for the same portfolio.[14]

A valuable perspective on the issue of risk management for alpha managers can be gained by considering the objectives of their investors. Over the years, most sophisticated investors have realized that asset allocation is the most critical factor in determining portfolio performance. Studies have shown that this decision accounts for as much as 90 percent of the return of a portfolio. Most of the time, large investors have determined their asset mix (say, 60 percent stocks and 40 percent bonds) before they consider the less important decision of which individual investment managers will be used to capture these returns.

By settling on an appropriate asset allocation, investors have accepted the risk associated with their chosen benchmarks. What investors are demanding, and what the active managers should be trying to deliver, is a superior risk-adjusted return above their given benchmark. So, for the investment manager the biggest risk is either achieving returns inferior to their benchmark or exposing the client to extraneous risk in the attempt to deliver benchmark returns.

Although neither of these issues is directly addressed by VaR, the tools needed to compare the risk and return attributes of an investment manager's portfolio relative to a benchmark have existed for more than 50 years. Called factor analysis, the technique attempts to uncover common sources of variability in return data. Factor models have been used to predict portfolio behavior, and in conjunction with other types of analysis, to construct customized portfolios with certain desired characteristics, such as the ability to track the performance of an index.

For example, suppose that an investor was interested in understanding the performance difference between an actively managed mutual fund and the S&P 500 index. The investor has no information about the portfolio construction of either investment. Armed solely with the historical performance of the two investments and a database of economic data, the market sector sensitivities of the two portfolios can be compared. Figure 11.1 shows that the actively managed portfolio has a larger exposure to financial, utility, and transportation stocks. In contrast, the S&P 500 index is weighted more in the technology, health care, and consumer products sectors. These sector weighting differences account for more than 96 percent of the difference between the advisor's return and that of the index.

Factor analysis can be quite useful in determining the biases of investment managers. In this example, the actively managed portfolio is concentrated more on value stocks than growth stocks. This bias can either be conscious (the manager feels that value stocks will outperform) or uncon-

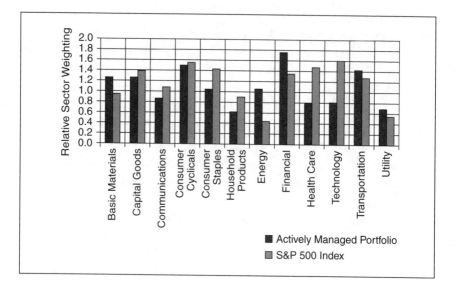

Figure 11.1   **Sector Exposures: Actively Managed Portfolio versus S&P 500 Index**

scious (past experiences in the markets might be influencing his stock selection). Regardless of intent, the increased sensitivity that biased portfolios frequently exhibit to changes in the business cycle or increased inflationary pressures often becomes apparent only after the fact. Unless these exposures are realized and controlled, the possibility of investment managers underperforming their benchmark during a difficult period is substantial.

$$\alpha$$

In many respects, the history of American whale hunting closely parallels the development of the investment management business. The first organized whaling in the American colonies began in New York in 1640. Using small rowboats, Colonial whalemen speared the beasts in the shallow beaches of the Northeast and extracted whale oil by boiling the blubber in large cast iron kettles called *trypots*. As the number of whales near shore inevitably declined, the colonists were forced to stalk their prey in deeper waters. Larger and more expensive boats had to be designed, and voyages ultimately lasted up to two years. Eventually, the whalemen were forced to go as far away as the Arctic Ocean for whales.

The decline of the whaling industry was almost exclusively a result of limited supply. Whales became so rare that the costs of finding them exceeded the revenues derived from selling whale oil and baleen. The last American whaling ships finally ceased operation in 1938.[15]

Does the business of alpha generation share the same fate as that of whaling? Will market inefficiencies become so difficult to find that research costs exceed revenues? Will alpha generation, like whaling, cease to be a viable business because of the lack of quarry?

Obviously, alpha generation has become more difficult with the passage of time. There is little doubt that investment skills have improved over the years, especially in the period since Harry Markowitz's seminal paper on risk and return. Yet when well-known investment consultant Peter Bernstein studied the return of portfolio managers from 1970 to present, he found that alpha generation over time has dissipated dramatically. There are two possible reasons for this observation. The first (and most obvious) explanation is that market efficiency has increased significantly over the time period studied, to the extent that it is nearly impossible to generate excess return.

The second and subtler rationale has to do with manager motivation. With the growing popularity of indexing, active managers have grown increasingly sensitive to *tracking error* risk (the risk of not achieving results comparable to a benchmark). The passion that institutional clients have with benchmarking has made large tracking errors extremely perilous for managers.[16] Thus, even if managers were able to construct an optimized portfolio—one that had the best return at a given level of risk—they may not implement it if the characteristics of the portfolio differed significantly from their benchmark. If this hypothesis is true, then with managers having no incentive to maximize returns, alpha generation over a benchmark like the S&P 500 would fall over time even among the best managers (Figure 11.2).[17]

In reality, both explanations hold some merit. If alpha generation is indeed getting more difficult, investment managers can take a number of steps to increase their likelihood of success. One of the most critical is to hold fast to a rigorous, defined method of hypothesis testing.

Science is based on two phenomena, which every scientist agrees are true: externality and corroboration. Externality is the perception that knowledge exists that has not been discovered. It describes the motivation of the scientific endeavor—to add to the body of understanding about natural systems. Corroboration is the tendency of our perceptions to reflect our preconceived notions about the world. What we assume to be true appears to be true. The scientific method is designed to foil corroboration, so that a researcher can see the world as it truly is—not merely how it appears to be.

A simplified version of the scientific method begins with market observation. A hypothesis is then formulated to explain what is causing the observation. The hypothesis must then be tested and the statistical significance of the results must be determined. If the results of the study are not conclusive, the hypothesis needs to be revised, the experiment was carried out incorrectly, or the analysis of the results was in error.

When applied to the social sciences like finance, the scientific method is *path dependent*. It is not enough to generate statistically pleasing

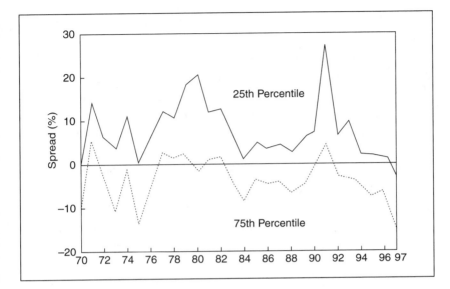

Figure 11.2 **Alpha Generation and Active Management, 1970–1997**

Vanishing edge? Since 1991, the top quartile of active managers has produced progressively less alpha over the S&P 500 index. The bottom quartile has also experienced diluted returns.

Source: Financial Analysts Journal, Nov. 2, 1998, p. 9. Copyright, 1998, *Financial Analysts Journal.* Reproduced and republished with permission from the Association for Investment and Management Research. All rights reserved. The Association for Investment and Management Research[SM] (AIMR[SM]) does not endorse, promote, review, or warrant the accuracy of the products or services offered by John Wiley & Sons.

results. If enough tests are performed, the odds favor that some false anomalies will be uncovered. For this reason, only those market inefficiencies that can be logically explained should be considered valid.

$$\alpha$$

Although oil production and renewable resource are not words that often appear together, something mysterious seems to be occurring in the oil fields off the coast of Louisiana. Production at Eugene Island 330, a large discovery found in 1973, peaked at 15,000 barrels per day (bpd), and in

1989 had slowed to less than 4,000 bpd. But suddenly—some would say almost inexplicably—Eugene Island's fortunes reversed. The field is now producing 13,000 bpd, and probable reserves have skyrocketed from 60 million barrels to more than 400 million barrels. This puzzling phenomenon has led some scientists to a radical theory—that Eugene Island is rapidly refilling itself, perhaps from some continuous source miles below the Earth's surface. This may indicate that oil may not be the limited resource it was once assumed to be.[18]

Like all natural systems, the capital markets have a tendency to act in an unpredictable fashion. As long as occasionally irrational people are around to program computers, it is unlikely that technological advances will result in perfectly efficient markets. And as long as market anomalies exist, there will be smart people around to exploit them.

Chapter 12

Alpha Respite III:
The Enigma of Asset Allocation

> Towering genius disdains a beaten path. It seeks regions
> hitherto unexplored.
>
> *Abraham Lincoln*

To Ludwig van Beethoven, life was a search for perfection. He was intolerant of the mediocre, the flawed, and the unexamined in both himself and in others. And like many great men, he conquered many obstacles to achieve his objective. When he first began to lose his hearing, a traumatic experience that would end the greatest of careers, Beethoven simply switched his emphasis from performing to composing. As his condition worsened, he often sat for hours writing music with his ear pressed to his piano so he could feel the vibrations of the notes.

Beethoven published his first symphony at the age of 31, a relatively late start for such a well-known composer. The reason for this delay has been traditionally explained by his respect for Wolfgang Amadeus Mozart and Joseph Haydn and his ambition to produce a work on equal terms with these symphonic masters. But an equally important reason was Beethoven's life philosophy, which was to accept nothing but the best. With tireless zeal, he reworked his compositions for years until he finally accepted them as the nearest thing to perfection that he could achieve.

Beethoven holds the distinction of never writing a flop. Alexander Wheelock Thayer, who kept musical criticism to an absolute minimum in his seminal work *The Life of Beethoven*, described one of his symphonies as "a work whose grand and imposing introduction . . . made it . . . a [defining moment] both in the life of its author and in the history of instrumental music."[1] Beethoven's nine symphonies and thirty-two piano sonatas remain essential study pieces for any serious student of music.

Winston Smith never thought of himself as a genius. Besides the great maestro, he thought of those minds that created modern financial theory. The word brought with it thoughts of Harry Markowitz, who developed modern portfolio theory and patiently waited 15 years for the investment establishment to embrace his ideas. William Sharpe, who transformed Markowitz's theory into a usable form by creating the capital asset pricing model, also popped into Smith's head. Smith considered himself merely a successful end user for all the great minds that came before him. He wondered if that were to suffice, as he was asked to solve one of the great riddles of investment theory.

It all began earlier that day, when Mr. Smith was invited to meet one of the most successful businessmen in the Southeast, Hari Seldon. Mr. Seldon's Atlanta-based venture capital business, PsychoHistory Investors (PSI), was one of the largest backers of technology start-up firms in the country. His books were perennial bestsellers and required reading in all of the top MBA programs. Mr. Smith was quite flattered at the invitation, which became even more enticing when he found out the location—on the tarmac of a fixed-base operator near Salisbury, North Carolina, aboard Mr. Seldon's Gulfstream III private jet.

Mr. Smith had modest expectations about the outcome of the meeting. In his mind, the best case scenario would have been to secure an investment for his market neutral fund. What he did not know was that one of Mr. Seldon's closest friends had been a client of Mr. Smith's for several years. Mr. Seldon was also acquainted with Kilgore Trout, a business associate of Mr. Smith's. Because of these relationships and his previous experiences with other investment professionals—a group that he considered rather uncreative and ill equipped—Mr. Seldon offered Mr. Smith's firm an unusual opportunity. Instead of committing to Mr. Smith that portion of his portfolio that would be dedicated to alternative investments (Mr. Smith's specialty), Mr. Seldon wanted him to invest $120 million on his behalf, which represented a sizable chunk of his net worth. The assets would be spread among several asset classes, including equities, fixed income, cash instruments, and alternative investments. The task that confronted Mr. Smith was to devise an asset allocation structure that would not only meet the objectives of his potential client, but also provide a meaningful alternative to the myriad of conventional investment plans that had been paraded in front of Mr. Seldon by the legions of bankers, brokers, and planners who desperately sought his business.

$$\alpha$$

If proof were ever needed that "the true artist creates out of his total experience," as the famed performer Denis Matthews once said, then one need only consider the circumstances surrounding the composition of Beethoven's Second Symphony. This brilliant and original piece was largely written during Beethoven's summer break in Heiligenstadt in 1802, at the time of his greatest despair concerning his increasing deafness. Beethoven had considered suicide as a way of solving his problem, and he wrote a letter to his brothers explaining the situation and asking forgiveness for his recent melancholy behavior. But he was destined to conquer his depression as successfully as his lack of hearing and soon returned to Vienna. The resulting symphony showcased Beethoven's humor, independence, and vitality. A critic present during the first performance described the new symphony typically, as "a work full of new, original ideas, of great strength, sensitive in orchestration and intellectual in concept."[2]

The opportunity to work with Mr. Seldon could not have come at a better time for Mr. Smith. Still smarting from the correction in August and September of 1998 that left his flagship product, the Smoky Mountain Market Neutral Fund, down for the year, Smith's firm desperately needed to land such a famous and well-respected client. But in order to do so, Mr. Smith had to devise a truly unique asset allocation structure, with a properly balanced historical view of the relationship of risk and return, but at the same time considering the occasional irrationality of investors, the high correlation of markets during crises, and the plethora of financially engineered investment products currently available. But in order to discover a new path, it was necessary to determine the direction that others took before him.

$$\alpha$$

Harry Markowitz started the revolution, when he proposed that the value of a security was dependent on three mathematical measures: the security's average return, its tendency to fluctuate (also known as its standard deviation), and its correlation with other securities. This heretical view amounted to ignoring a lot of fundamental information about a company—its earnings, its dividend policy, and its competitors, to name a few—and to instead focus on a few simple calculations. The relationship between a security's risk and return can then be easily represented on a two-dimensional graph as in Figure 12.1.

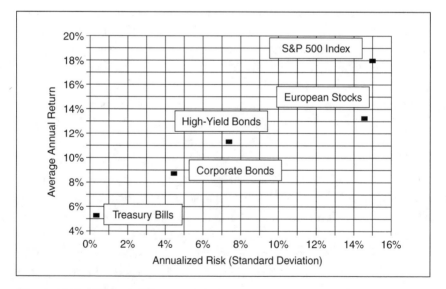

Figure 12.1   **Risk and Return**

Modern portfolio theory (MPT) suggests that investments with high relative rates of return are riskier than those investments with lower returns.

In Markowitz's realm, no single asset class dominates all others. As return increases, so does risk. The decision as to which investment is appropriate varies according to the risk tolerance of the individual. An investor who preferred a low-risk strategy would choose the asset class with a small standard deviation, since the value of that security is likely to fluctuate very little. More aggressive investors with a higher threshold for risk could choose assets with higher returns.

Now instead of being restricted to a given investment, suppose one could choose between holding a mix of different assets and the weighting of each investment could be varied. The series of dots on the page suddenly becomes a curve (Figure 12.2). Each point on this curve, which is called the efficient frontier, represents the portfolio that delivers the highest possible return for a given level of risk. The point at the apex of the curve represents the portfolio that gives investors the optimum bang for their buck. It boasts the highest ratio of return to risk of any asset mix.

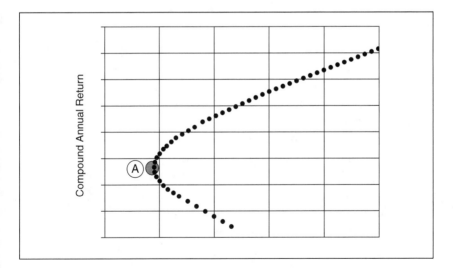

Figure 12.2   **Annualized Standard Deviation**
The efficient frontier. The graph from point A and above represents portfolios with the highest return at a given level of risk (or standard deviation). Point A represents the market portfolio, which yields the best ratio of return and risk.

Markowitz's innovations brought with them numerous philosophical debates. How does one best use the efficient frontier? Should investors with dissimilar risk tolerances hold different portfolios? This question was answered by economist James Tobin in 1958. Tobin showed that the decision about how much risk to take is a totally separate one from the decision about which investments to own. Everyone, according to Tobin, should own the optimum portfolio. If the optimal portfolio is too risky for an investor, he should allocate only a portion of their total assets to it, and invest the balance in risk-free Treasury bills or a bank savings account. If the portfolio is too tame for other investors, they could increase their exposure through the use of borrowed funds. In any case, only the optimal mix of investments—the one that gives the highest proportion of return to risk—should be considered.

According to Tobin, that optimal portfolio is not a secret, complex mixture of securities, locked in a safe and protected by sentries. Rather, it is "the market"—the range of all available investments—taken in its entirety. Peter Bernstein's excellent book *Capital Ideas* captures the mindset of the California Public Employees Retirement System (or CalPERS, as it is known in the investment community), which invests more than $20 billion in-house with the notion that the "market portfolio" is indeed the only one to consider:

> The army of security analysts researching individual stocks has disappeared, because CalPERS holds a convenient replica of the market portfolio. The outside managers earning handsome fees have lost the System as a client, because their decision would be redundant. The brokerage community no longer wins fat commissions, because the System's traders feel no urgency to buy or sell any particular stock, preferring to let the market come to them. The System frequently trades electronically with other large investors, bypassing Wall Street altogether.[3]

Markowitz's work also introduced a technical dilemma. Because of the enormous number of calculations involved, it was very difficult for a practitioner to utilize his new concepts. In 1960, Markowitz encouraged a young Ph.D. student named William F. Sharpe to further investigate this new field of portfolio theory. Sharpe's innovation was to link returns to a single risk factor, which eventually became known as the capital asset pricing model (CAPM).

Every investment carried two distinct risks, the CAPM explains. One is the risk of being invested in the market, which Sharpe called *systematic risk*. This risk, later referred to as the Greek symbol "beta" (or β), cannot be diversified away. The other, called *unsystematic risk*, is specific to a company's fortunes. Since this uncertainty can be mitigated through appropriate diversification, Sharpe figured that a portfolio's expected return is dependent solely on its beta, which measures its relationship to the overall market. In short, the CAPM helps measure the risk an investor is taking, and gauges the amount of return an investor can expect for taking that risk (Figure 12.3).[4]

For their efforts, Markowitz, Tobin, and Sharpe are Nobel laureates, which underscores the importance of their work. Virtually all portfolio

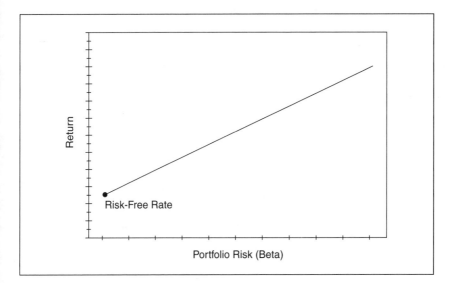

Figure 12.3   **Beta and Returns**
According to the capital asset pricing model (CAPM), the relationship between portfolio risk (or beta) and return should be linear.

managers today utilize some sort of portfolio optimization software in their decision making. Its utility in the evaluation of basic risk and return trade-offs is invaluable.

The key to developing an adjunct theory, thought Mr. Smith, lay in examining the assumptions used to develop this approach. In order to reflect the cogent realities of investing, he must find wrinkles that can be better explained than when Markowitz first began nearly 50 years ago.

α

One of the more universal mathematical assumptions used in science is that data follows a normal distribution. The normal distribution was first observed by Abraham de Moivre, a French mathematician, in his 1733 treatise *The Doctrine of Chances*. De Moivre's work showed that a set of random numbers would distribute themselves around their average value. The normal curve shows that the largest number of observations cluster around the center, close to the average of the total number of observations (Figure 12.4). The curve then slopes symmetrically downward, with an equal number of observations on either side of the mean, descending steeply at first and then exhibiting a flatter downward slope at each end. In other words, observations far from the mean are less frequent than observations close to the mean.[5]

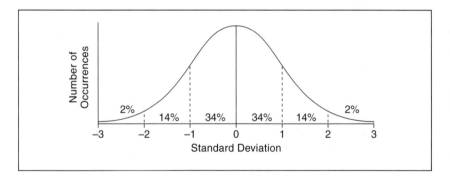

Figure 12.4   **Standard Deviation**
Data that conform to a normal distribution tend to center around the average measurement. The standard deviation of the data indicates the likelihood of an extreme data point.

The normal distribution is also referred to as being Gaussian, after the great mathematician Carl Friedrich Gauss. A true child prodigy, Gauss taught himself to read and write at the age of three. In 1807, as the French army was approaching his home in Göttingen, Napoleon ordered his troops to spare the city because "the greatest mathematician of all times is living there."[6] Gauss became enamored with statistics when he was asked to complete a geodesic survey of his home country of Bavaria. This type of survey, which measures the curvature of the Earth to improve the accuracy of geographic measures, requires extensive fieldwork. As Gauss analyzed his results, he found that they clustered around a central point. The more measurements Gauss took, the clearer the picture became and the more it resembled the bell curve that de Moivre had found 83 years earlier.[7] This discovery allowed him to take fewer measurements and to complete his job in less time, but with no loss of accuracy. Gauss's devotion to the science of statistics served him well. His application of statistics to the world of investing made him a successful speculator, and he died in 1855 a rich man.

Many natural processes follow a normal distribution. Reading ability, job satisfaction, and physical attributes like height and weight tend to follow the bell curve. This allows scientists to utilize variables like the average and the standard deviation, which tells them where data points are most likely to be clustered. When data does not conform to a normal distribution, other types of statistical tests have to be used. Unfortunately, these tests often lack the power of parametric statistics and require inference and explanation.

Unlike Gauss' geodesic measurements, historical stock price data is quite easy to obtain. When these prices are compiled on a graph called a histogram, they closely resemble the normal distribution, but with one important exception. Extreme observations—abnormally large positive and negative returns—occur with much larger frequency than the bell curve suggests. Thus, the stock market can be a much more dangerous place than would otherwise appear, because the odds of a big loss are often underestimated (Figure 12.5).

To make matters worse, correlation coefficients, which tell whether different markets move in unison or opposite to one another, often

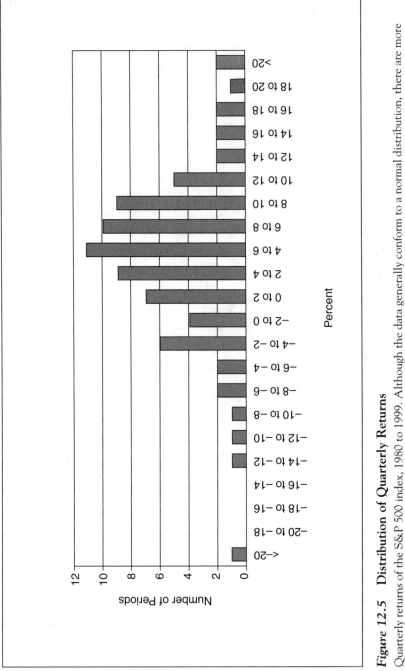

Figure 12.5   **Distribution of Quarterly Returns**

Quarterly returns of the S&P 500 index, 1980 to 1999. Although the data generally conform to a normal distribution, there are more outliers—quarters of large gains or losses—than would be expected.

become unstable when an outlier occurs. If the U.S. stock market crashes, for example, the odds of a meltdown in Tokyo, Singapore, London, Paris, and Mexico City are high, even though these markets move independently during normal conditions. Thus, even the most diversified of portfolios are at risk during market turmoil.

One way to avoid such trouble is to evaluate the amount of data fed into optimization programs. For instance, an investor in early 1998 who was interested in constructing a broadly diversified portfolio that included arbitrage strategies would likely run a Markowitz optimization with returns starting in late 1994 or early 1995, the date that many of these funds were launched. Such an optimization would also include performance information on a variety of stock indices (both global and domestic), bonds (government, corporate, high-yield, and international), and perhaps real estate investment trusts (REITs) and mortgage-backed securities. The results of this optimization would suggest a relatively high allocation to arbitrageurs, because during this period their funds boasted impressive returns with very low volatility that were not correlated with traditional investments.

The optimization would fail to consider several crucial issues. First, an optimization over such a short time frame does not include early 1994—a period of rising interest rates, when many arb funds sustained heavy losses. Second, the limited time window of the study masks the tendency of arb funds to lose money when stocks and bonds investments are likewise unprofitable. Our hapless investor will likely not achieve the type of diversification he was looking for. The most obvious solution to this problem is simply to include more data in the optimization process. But that is often not possible, since many hedge funds have a limited operating history.

A more pragmatic approach is to consider the results of such an optimization with a large grain of salt. Since alternative investments are much more dependent on manager skill than on the returns of an asset class, it is important to weigh qualitative factors such as the advisor's infrastructure, quality of staff, and firm capitalization. Diversification—the utilization of a multiple hedge-fund approach—is also important. Finally, ongoing due diligence and frequent contact with the manager is invaluable in determining if the advisor is sticking to his or her specialty, or is being forced by an influx of capital to explore other strategies.

One might also consider investments that are designed to profit from the chaos associated with market downturns. These periods often portend pronounced trends in the foreign exchange markets, which can be profitably exploited by currency managers. Managed futures have also been shown to be the most profitable during periods of extreme stock market duress, while still maintaining profitability during normal market conditions.

α

Another area that interested Mr. Smith was the concept of rationality. Markowitz's work hinged on the behavior of risk-adverse investors, whose appetite for risk diminishes as their wealth increases. This type of investor prefers a sure amount to a wager with the same expected value. And according to theory, a rational investor's buy and sell decisions in the markets should be independent of his or her previous success or failure.

But people are not always rational. Our behavior often depends more on our most recent past experiences than on the desire to maximize our utility (or satisfaction). Noted behavioral researchers Amos Tversky and Daniel Kahneman illustrated the human tendency to consistently act in an unreasonable fashion in a famous experiment. They posed the following two scenarios to a large group of people and recorded their answers.

In the first problem, the participants were asked to pretend that they have been given $1,000. They were then asked to choose between two alternatives:

A. A sure gain of $500
B. A 50 percent chance to gain $1,000 and a 50 percent chance to gain nothing.

The researchers found that 84 percent of subjects preferred A. The predominant choice of the sure amount over the gamble is consistent with risk aversion because the expected value of the gamble is no greater than the sure amount of the payoff.

The second problem was similar to the first, except that the subjects were told they were given $2,000. They were then asked to choose between the following alternatives:

C. A sure loss of $500
D. A 50 percent chance to lose $1,000 and a 50 percent chance to lose nothing.

A majority of subjects chose D, the gamble, in this scenario. Kahneman and Tversky described the motivation for D as an aversion to losses. The desire to avoid the sure loss of $500 drives investors to accept the possibility of losing $1,000 in the hopes of breaking even.[8]

The experiment also shows that investors act as if they are risk averse when they are making profitable decisions, but will embrace risk in the avoidance of an unprofitable decision (Figure 12.6). If this result is the norm for the typical investor, the standard assumptions about investor behavior made by Markowitz and Sharpe lack complete accuracy.

Although at first amused by these findings, Mr. Smith reminded himself that he occasionally delayed the decision to dump a poorly performing hedge fund, in the hope that the fund would recover some of the losses before termination. Thinking that there might be a way to profit from such a persistent predilection, Mr. Smith asked the quant jocks to find more research on the subject.

Mr. Smith was surprised to find a plethora of well-written studies on behavioral tendencies. A recently published paper in *American Economic Review* was particularly noteworthy.[9] The study analyzed the trading habits of retail investors with discount brokerage accounts. These individuals were attracted to two kinds of stocks. The first were those high-flying issues that have experienced a pronounced uptrend—the so-called momentum stocks. While it is certainly feasible to purchase these types of equities (and there is academic research that supports such a strategy), the retail investors in this study waited until these stocks had risen for two years to initiate a position.

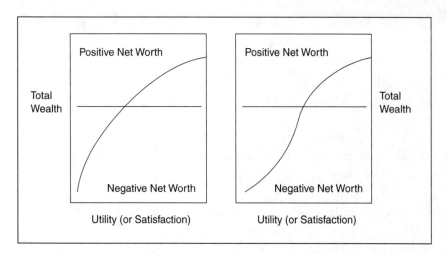

Figure 12.6   Utility Curves

The curve at left shows that a person's utility slowly rises as total wealth increases. Such an investor is always averse to risk. At right, an investor is risk seeking when facing a loss, but risk averse when profitable. The work of Markowitz and Sharpe are based on the former. The latter curve has been shown to be more reflective of human behavior by researchers.

Unfortunately, stocks that outperform the market for a considerable amount of time (i.e., more than 12 months) are likely to experience a reversal. If the rise of momentum securities is due, in part, to the purchases of momentum traders, then the last momentum trader to take a position may be the first to suffer losses when the trend reverses. Indeed, some of the underperformance of the securities held by the investors in the study may be due to the mistiming of momentum cycles.[10]

The second group of stocks favored by the investors in the study were those that experienced substantial depreciation. These issues could be considered "value" stocks, because this depreciation put the price of the stock either below or very close to the book value of the company. Like the predilection for momentum stocks, the purchase of value stocks is supported by both behavioral research (Richard Thaler, Josef Lakonishok) and historical precedent (i.e., John Maynard Keynes, Ben Graham). Considering their lack of success with momentum stocks, Mr. Smith wondered if the investors in the study were more profitable when playing the role of value investors.

Mr. Smith was disappointed in learning that although retail investors preferred to *buy* two different types of stocks—momentum and value—their *selling* habits were quite uniform. The individuals had a tendency to exit profitable positions if the price of a stock appreciated substantially in the two weeks that followed their purchase. However, stocks whose price fell were usually held, presumably in the hope that the stock's price would rebound and the position could be exited. These results exactly mirror the findings of Kahneman and Tversky. In both instances, the tendency for people to realize gains is strong, but when facing a loss, they are more likely to risk increasing the loss for a chance that the stock's price will rebound. But perhaps the most surprising result was that the securities purchased and held consistently underperformed those that were sold (Figure 12.7).

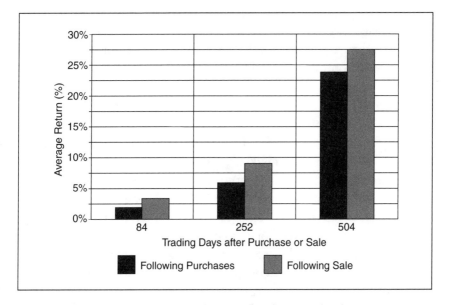

Figure 12.7   **Average Returns Following Purchases and Sales**
Individual investors typically sell those stocks that significantly appreciate in the two weeks following their purchase, while keeping those stocks that depreciate. As a result, the stock positions maintained in their portfolios tend to underperform those that they liquidate.
Source: Based on data from T. Odean, "Do Investors Trade Too Much?" *American Economic Review,* 1999.

Is it possible, wondered Mr. Smith, to profit by reversing the self-destructive behavior of these investors? If that were the case, he should seek investment advisors with two distinct niches. The first were those managers who exploited the tendency for stocks to exhibit momentum, but only in the short term (i.e., less than a one-year holding period). The other managers of interest would have a value orientation, but would sell those issues that did not benefit from information releases (such as quarterly earnings reports) that were generally positive and caused price appreciation. In both instances, Mr. Smith should look for managers who are quick to take a loss, but patient in their generation of unrealized gains.

Of course, in order for Mr. Smith to consider any managers that utilize these strategies, they must show an ability to produce excess returns over their stated benchmark. Particular emphasis would be shown to those managers willing to be compensated based on performance. And since these managers would likely produce more turnover (and thus more realized gains) than a traditional index fund, Mr. Smith would utilize them in the nontaxed portion of Mr. Seldon's assets.

$$\alpha$$

One final piece of the CAPM puzzle interested Mr. Smith. According to Tobin and Sharpe, the "market" portfolio is the combination of assets that yields the highest ratio of return to risk. Since this portfolio is the most efficient investment available, it is the only one that a rational investor should consider. If the return of this portfolio is too tame for one investor, Tobin's separation theorem suggests, then one could simply borrow money to increase his or her exposure to risky assets. Similarly, a more risk adverse investor would only commit a portion of his assets to the portfolio and place the balance in a risk-free Treasury bill or savings account.

In equilibrium (the state where the number of buyers and sellers are the same), every security must be part of the market portfolio. If a security were not included, there would be an absence of buyers, causing its price to drop. The resulting lower price would cause the expected return of the security to rise until the optimization program recognized its existence and included it in the portfolio.

This concept, thought Mr. Smith, must apply not only to securities but also to different market strategies. For instance, a lack of arbitrage activity in the U.S. government debt market would cause bond pricing efficiency to drop significantly. Bond arbitrage would then enjoy renewed profitability and would likely attract both new participants and a fresh influx of capital. This is similar to what happened after the third quarter of 1998, when a number of arbitrage firms were shuttered due to the enormous volatility in the global debt markets.

All investors, reckoned Mr. Smith, are part of a mechanism that constantly adjusts prices to their fair value. A lack of buyers in one strategy or asset class can create profitable opportunities to those who are both liquid and knowledgeable. Conversely, a huge influx of capital to any given market sector could create such an efficient marketplace that a reversal of fortunes becomes imminent. In the words of Peter Bernstein, the consulting editor of the *Journal of Portfolio Management*:

> Is there such a thing as an equilibrium price in the real world? Equilibrium means a state of rest in which nothing moves unless and until some force from outside the system arrives upon the scene. Equilibrium is the ultimate destination to which cause and effect are leading. Once equilibrium is reached, the cause has exhausted itself, and the effect is complete; by definition, everything is now in balance and stands still.
>
> Nothing in life stands still! Equilibrium is a state of nature that can only exist in the absence of uncertainty, only in a static rather than a dynamic environment, only when agents make decisions on the basis of perfect foresight. If disagreement or imperfect or incomplete information exists, the price cannot stand still, and there is no equilibrium. Yet that is the quality of all the information that we have to process. Once the future is the least bit cloudy, equilibrium vanishes.[11]

α

During the Renaissance, the efforts of scientists centered around finding the proverbial Holy Grail, or that which could explain everything easily and with little human effort. Today, that quest continues. Scientists have tried for years to formulate a theory that could unify the four known interactions—gravity, electromagnetism, and the strong and weak nuclear forces. Albert Einstein thought that if he could find the right unified field theory, he would finally understand the structure of matter.

Over the years Einstein proposed unified field theories in various mathematical forms. Flaws were detected in his theories one by one, usually by Einstein himself. Undaunted, he would try new formulations, only to see them fail in turn. "One cannot help but be in awe when one contemplates the mysteries of eternity, of life, and of the marvelous structure of reality," he wrote. "It is enough if one tries merely to comprehend a little of this mystery each day."[12]

In developing a unified investment theory, Mr. Smith would have to consider the four known forces—transaction costs, risk, return, and market efficiency. He knew that the ultimate portfolio would minimize the first two, maximize the third, and find its way around the last. Taxes and liquidity concerns would only serve to make the model even more complex.

Mr. Smith was aware that mathematics could easily solve 70 to 80 percent of the puzzle, and that anyone with simple computing skills could at least get that far. But the balance of the enigma could only be approached through intuition, experience, and gut instinct.

Investing, he thought, was art. Science merely helped in the mixture of the paint, not on its application to the canvas.

Notes

Chapter 1—The Equation That Changed the Investment World

1. George Katona, *Psychological Economics* (New York: Elsevier, 1975), pp. 267–270.
2. Peter Bernstein, *Capital Ideas* (New York: The Free Press, 1992), p. 46.
3. John B. Williams, *The Theory of Investment Value* (Cambridge, MA: Harvard University Press, 1938), p. 5.
4. Bernstein, *Capital Ideas*, p. 47.
5. Shlomo Maital, *Minds, Markets, and Money* (New York: Basic Books, 1982), p. 200.
6. Edwin J. Elton and Martin J. Gruber, *Modern Portfolio Theory and Investment Analysis* (New York: John Wiley & Sons, 1987), p. 193.
7. Ibid.
8. Maital, *Minds, Markets, and Money*, p. 215.
9. Ibid.
10. John M. Keynes, *The General Theory of Employment, Interest, and Money* (New York: Harcourt, Brace & Co., 1936), p. 75.
11. Burton G. Malkiel. *A Random Walk Down Wall Street* (New York: W. W. Norton, 1996), p. 32.
12. Keynes, *General Theory*, p. 77.
13. Gerald M. Loeb, *The Battle for Investment Survival* (New York: John Wiley & Sons, 1996), p. 168.
14. Bernstein, *Capital Ideas*, p. 83.
15. Ray Harrod, *The Life of John Maynard Keynes* (New York: W. W. Norton, 1951), p. 401.
16. The Nobel Foundation, The Nobel Foundation website. (www.nobel.se), 1997.

17. Ibid.

18. James Tobin, "Liquidity Preference as Behavior Towards Risk." *Review of Economic Studies*, Vol. 67, pp. 65–86 (1958).

19. William Briet and Roger W. Spencer, eds., *Lives of the Laureates: Seven Nobel Economists* (Cambridge, MA: MIT Press, 1986), pp. 113–136.

20. William F. Sharpe, "A Simplified Model for Portfolio Analysis." *Management Science*, Vol. 9, pp. 277–293 (1962).

21. Malkiel, *Random Walk*, p. 242.

22. Ibid.

23. Malkiel, *Random Walk*, p. 257.

Chapter 2—The Revolution of Index-Based Investing

1. Peter Bernstein, *Capital Ideas* (New York: The Free Press, 1992), p. 20.

2. Paul Samuelson, "Challenge to Judgment." *Journal of Portfolio Management* (Fall 1974).

3. Eugene F. Fama, "Efficient Capital Markets: A Review of Theory and Empirical Work." *Journal of Finance*, Vol. 25, No. 2, pp. 383–417 (May 1970).

4. Ibid.

5. William A. Sherden, *The Fortune Sellers* (New York: John Wiley & Sons, 1998), p. 92.

6. Dean LeBaron, *The Ins and Outs of Institutional Investing*. Dean LeBaron website (www.deanlebaron.com), 1998, Chapter 3, p. 1.

7. Ibid.

8. Samuelson, "Challenge to Judgment."

9. Ibid.

10. Bernstein, 1992, p. 248.

11. E. F. Ehrbar, "Indexing: An Idea Whose Time Has Come." *Fortune*, June 1976, p. 144.

12. Ibid.

13. John C. Bogle, *Investing with Simplicity*. Keynote speech, The Intelligent Investing Conference, The Philadelphia Inquirer, Philadelphia, PA, Oct. 3, 1998.
14. Ibid.
15. Ibid.
16. James Picerno, "Bull Market Blues." *Dow Jones Asset Management*, May 6, 1998, pp. 32–38.
17. Ibid.
18. Ibid.
19. Ibid.
20. Ibid.
21. Michael Fritz, "Bond Index Funds Wield Better Yields." *Investment-News*, Nov. 5, 1999, p. 24.
22. Ibid.

Chapter 3—Can Anyone Outperform the Market?

1. Brown, 1999, pp. 94–102.
2. Ned Downing, "Revolutionary Idea." *Barron's*, April 15, 1999, pp. 29–30.
3. Carole Gould, "Poof! For More and More Mutual Funds, A Quick Disappearing Act." *New York Times*, Aug. 16, 1998, p. 11.
4. Hal Lux and Jack Willoughby, "May Day II." *Institutional Investor*, Jan. 1999, pp. 45–46.
5. Ibid.
6. Ibid.
7. Ibid.
8. Ken Brown, "The Reckoning." *Smart Money*, Feb. 1999, p. 98.
9. Walton Taylor and James Yoder, "Mutual Fund Trading Activity and Investor Utility." *Financial Analyst Journal*, May 6, 1994, pp. 66–69.
10. James Picerno, "Bull Market Blues." *Dow Jones Asset Management*, May 6, 1998, pp. 29–30.

11. John Khin, "To Load or Not to Load: A Study of the Marketing and Distribution Charges of Mutual Funds." *Financial Analysts Journal*, May 6, 1996, pp. 28–36.
12. Richard McEnally and Carl Ackerman, "The Returns of Hedge Funds: Risk, Return, and Incentives." *Journal of Finance* (1999, forthcoming).

Chapter 4—Alpha Respite I: The Case of the Tempted Money Manager

1. Andre F. Perold and Robert S. Salomon, Jr. "The Right Amount of Assets Under Management." *Financial Analysts Journal*, May 6, 1991, pp. 31–39.
2. Ibid.
3. Ibid.
4. Hal Lux, "Hedge Fund? Who, Me?" *Institutional Investor*, August 1998, p. 36.

Chapter 5—Arbitrage and Other "Free" Lunches

1. "The History of Football." NFL website (www.nflhistory.com), 1998.
2. Ron Neyer, "Breaking Down NFC Superiority." *ESPN Sports Zone*, Jan. 17, 1997; ESPN website (www.espn.go.com).
3. Charles Ellis, *Investment Policy* (Chicago: Dow Jones Irwin, 1985), p. 13.
4. Gordon Thomas and Max Morgan-Witts, *The Day the Bubble Burst* (New York: Doubleday & Co., 1908), p. 268.
5. John Kenneth Galbraith, *The Great Crash of 1929* (Cambridge, MA: Riverside Press, 1961), p. 90.
6. William Sherden, *The Fortune Sellers* (New York: John Wiley & Sons, 1998), p. 97.
7. Galbraith, *The Great Crash of 1929*, p. 90.
8. Ibid., pp. 64–68.
9. Michael Lewis, *Liar's Poker* (New York: Penguin Books, 1990), p. 142.

10. Michael Lewis, "How the Eggheads Cracked." *New York Times Magazine*, Jan. 24, 1999, pp. 24–42.
11. Robert McGough and Steve Liesman, "Wall Street Leaves Billions on the Table in Oil Mergers." *Wall Street Journal*, May 11, 1999, p. C1.

Chapter 6—Enhancements to CAPM: The Search for Financial DNA

1. Isaac Cronin and Raphael Pallais, *Champagne!* (New York: Pocket Books, 1985), pp. 10–12.
2. Desmond Seward, *Monks and Wine* (New York: Crown Publishing, 1979), p. 140.
3. Ibid.
4. Peter Bernstein, *Against the Gods: The Remarkable Story of Risk* (New York: John Wiley & Sons, 1996), p. 258.
5. Peter Bernstein, *Capital Ideas* (New York: The Free Press, 1992), p. 127.
6. Shawn Tully, "How the Smart Money Really Invests." *Money*, July 6, 1998.
7. Ibid.
8. John Rekenthaler, "The Long Wait." *Dow Jones Asset Management*, Jan. 2, 1999, pp. 31–36.
9. Eugene F. Fama and Kenneth French, "Multifactor Explanations of Asset Pricing Anomalies." *Journal of Finance*, Vol. 51, pp. 55–84, 1996.
10. Tully, "Smart Money."
11. Ibid.
12. My apologies to Sharpe et al.
13. Eugene Fama, "Value versus Growth: The International Evidence." *Journal of Finance*, Vol. 53, No. 6 (Dec. 1998).
14. Jonathon Burton, "Mispricing and Unrealistic Expectations." *Dow Jones Asset Management*, March 4, 1999, pp. 21–28.
15. John Blin, "Arbitrage Pricing Theory." Applied Portfolio Technology, LTD website (www.aptltd.com), 1999.

16. John Blin, "Risk for the Mathematically Disinclined." *Derivatives Strategy*, May 1997, pp. 40–41.
17. Saul Hansell, "Inside Morgan Stanley's Black Box." *Institutional Investor*, May 1989, pp. 204–216.

Chapter 7—Managed Futures and Portable Alpha

1. The Nobel Foundation website (www.nobel.se.), 1997.
2. Donald L. Horowitz and Robert J. Mackay, "Derivatives: State of the Debate," in Richard Teweles, Frank Jones, and Ben Warwick, eds., *The Futures Game* (Chicago: McGraw Hill, 1999), p. 16.
3. Richard Teweles, Frank Jones, and Ben Warwick, eds. *The Futures Game* (Chicago: McGraw Hill, 1999), p. 9.
4. Ibid., p. 11.
5. Jerry W. Markham, *The History of Commodity Futures Trading and Its Regulation* (New York: Praeger, 1987), pp. 5–6.
6. Ibid., pp. 39–42.
7. Eugene Fama and M. Blume, "Filter Rules and Stock Market Trading Profits." *Journal of Business*, Vol. 39, pp. 226–241 (1966).
8. Hal Lux, "Extreme Finance." *Institutional Investor*, Oct. 1998, pp. 45–49.
9. Roy Niederhoffer, "Hedge Against What?" *Barron's*, Feb. 1, 1999.
10. Institutional Investor Forum, "Mainstreaming Derivatives." *Institutional Investor*, Aug. 1999, p. 160.
11. Robert T. Carroll, "Occam's Razor." *Skeptic's Dictionary* website (1994–1999).

Chapter 8—Alpha Respite II: The Case of the Converging Correlations

1. Jess Lederman and Robert A. Klein, eds. *Market Neutral: State of the Art Strategies for Every Market Environment* (New York: McGraw Hill, 1996), p. 18.
2. Ibid., p. 20.

3. Edward Chancellor, *Devil Take the Hindmost: A History of Financial Speculation* (New York: Farrar Strauss Giroux, 1999), pp. 337–345.
4. Michael Lewis, "How the Eggheads Cracked." *New York Times Magazine*, Jan. 24, 1999, pp. 24–42.
5. United Press Syndicate, Calvin and Hobbes website (www.calvinandhobbes.com), 1999.
6. Ibid.
7. Ibid.
8. Putnam, 1998a.
9. Ibid.
10. Tal Cohen, Tal Cohen's Bookshelf (www.forum2.org/tal/books), 1998.

Chapter 9—Alpha Generation and Taxes

1. Robert H. Jeffrey and Robert D. Arnott, "Is Your Alpha Big Enough to Cover Its Taxes?" *Journal of Portfolio Management*, Spring 1993, pp. 15–25. The bulk of this chapter is based on this landmark work.
2. Jonathan Clements, "How the Taxman Dines on Your Mutual Fund." *Wall Street Journal*, Aug. 31, 1999, p. C1.
3. Jeffrey and Arnott, "Is Your Alpha Big Enough?" pp. 15–25.
4. Heritage Foundation, "The History of Taxation." The Heritage Foundation website (www.taxation.org), 1998
5. E. S. Browning, "Where There's a Tax Cut, Wall Street Finds a Way." *Wall Street Journal*, Oct. 27, 1997, p. C1.
6. Robert McIntyre, "Tax Shelters: The Video Game." *Slate*, Oct. 24, 1997.
7. Tom Herman, "Tax Report." *Wall Street Journal*, Sept. 8, 1999, p. A1.
8. Browning, "Where There's a Tax Cut," p. C1.

Chapter 10—Behavioral Finance: Are We Really That Irrational?

1. John Harvey, "Heuristic Judgment Theory." The University of Colorado website (www.csf.colorado.edu), 1996, p. 1.

2. William Gallacher, *Winner Take All* (Chicago: Probus, 1994), pp. 67–68.
3. Dean LeBaron, *The Ins and Outs of Institutional Investing.* Dean LeBaron website (www.deanlebaron.com), 1998, Chapter 2, p. 4.
4. Tony Lawson and Hashem Pesaran, eds. *Keynesian Economics* (Armonk, NY: M. E. Sharpe, 1985), pp. 46–65.
5. Hal Lux, "Extreme Finance." *Institutional Investor*, Oct. 1998, pp. 45–49.
6. Michael Reltz, "Winner's Curse." *Worth Magazine*, Feb. 1999.
7. Ibid.
8. Investor Home, The Investor Home website (www.investorhome.com), 1999.
9. Narashimhan Jagadesh and Sheridan Titman, "Returns to Buying Winners and Selling Losers: Implications for Stock Market Efficiency." *Journal of Finance*, Vol. 48, pp. 65–91 (1993).
10. Eugene F. Fama and Kenneth French, "Multifactor Explanations of Asset Pricing Anomalies." *Journal of Finance*, Vol. 51, pp. 55–84 (1996).
11. Harrison Hong, Terrence Lim, and Jeremy Stein, "Bad News Travels Slowly: Size Analyst Coverage, and the Profitability of Momentum Strategies." *Journal of Finance* (1998, forthcoming).
12. Ibid.
13. Ibid.
14. Gustave LeBon and Charles Mackay, *The Crowd and Extraordinary Popular Delusions* (Greenville, NC: Traders Press, 1994), pp. 274–284.
15. E. F. Ehrbar, "Indexing: An Idea Whose Time Has Come." *Fortune*, June 1976, p. 144.
16. Ibid.
17. Ibid.
18. Ibid.
19. LeBon and Mackay, *The Crowd and Extraordinary Delusions*, pp. 274–284.

20. John Bogle, *Investing with Simplicity*. Keynote speech, The Intelligent Investing Conference, The Philadelphia Inquirer, Philadelphia, PA, Oct. 3, 1998.
21. Edward Chancellor, *Devil Take the Hindmost: A History of Financial Speculation* (New York: Farrar Strauss Giroux, 1999), p. 151.
22. Ibid.
23. Jason Zweig, "Confessions of a Fund Pro." *Money*, Feb. 1999, pp. 73–75.

Chapter 11—Technology and the Capital Markets

1. Daniel Yergin, *The Prize* (New York: Simon and Schuster, 1991), p. 82.
2. Peter Coy, "Mining Profits from Microdata." *Business Week*, Dec. 1, 1997.
3. James Picerno, "Alarming Efficiency." *Institutional Investor*, May 6, 1999, pp. 43–48.
4. Ibid.
5. Massimo Pitatelli-Palmarino, *Inevitable Illusions: How Mistakes of Reason Rule Our Minds* (New York: John Wiley & Sons, 1994).
6. Ibid.
7. Ibid.
8. Picerno, "Alarming Efficiency," pp. 43–48.
9. Andrew Lo and A. Craig MacKinley, *A Non-Random Walk Down Wall Street* (Princeton, NJ: Princeton University Press, 1999), p. 186.
10. *Asia Week*, "Billion Dollar Man." Dec. 29, 1995, p. 17.
11. Christopher Culp, Ron Mensink, and Andrea Neves, "Value at Risk for Asset Managers." *Derivatives Weekly* (1999, forthcoming).
12. Bluford Putnam, "Risk Management for Banks and Funds Is Not the Same Game." *Global Investor*, Sept. 1998.
13. Bluford Putnam, "An Investment Paradigm for the New Millennium." *Global Investor*, Nov. 1997.

14. Tanya Beder, "VaR: Seductive But Dangerous." *Financial Analysts Journal*, Sept. 10, 1995, pp. 12–24.
15. New Bedford Whaling Museum, The History of Whaling website (www.whalingmuseum.org), 1999.
16. Peter Bernstein, "Where, Oh Where Are the .400 Hitters of Yesteryear?" *Financial Analysts Journal*, Nov. 2, 1998, pp. 6–14.
17. Ibid.
18. Christopher Cooper, "It's No Crude Joke: This Oil Field Grows Even as It's Tapped." *Wall Street Journal*, Nov. 12,1999, p. A1.

Chapter 12—Alpha Respite III: The Enigma of Asset Allocation

1. Po-Han Lin, The Beethoven Depot website (www.edepot.com), 1996.
2. Ibid.
3. Peter Bernstein, *Capital Ideas* (New York: The Free Press, 1992), p. 193.
4. Ibid.
5. University of St. Andrews, The History of Mathematics website (www-history.mcs.st-andrews.ac.uk), 1997.
6. Ibid.
7. Ibid.
8. Kenneth Fisher and Meir Statman, "A Behavioral Framework for Time Diversification." *Financial Analysts Journal*, May 6, 1999, pp. 87–99.
9. Terrance Odean, "Do Investors Trade Too Much?" *American Economic Review* (1999, forthcoming).
10. Ibid.
11. Peter Bernstein, "A New Look at the Efficient Market Hypothesis." *Journal of Portfolio Management*, Vol. 25, p. 1 (Winter 1999).
12. American Institute of Physics, "Science and Philosophy II." American Institute of Physics website (www.aip.org/history), 2000.

Bibliography

American Institute of Physics. 2000. "Science and Philosophy II." American Institute of Physics website (www.aip.org/history).

Asia Week. 1995. "Billion Dollar Man." Dec. 29, p. 17.

Asimov, Isaac. 1991. *Foundation.* New York: Bantam Books.

Atlas, Riva. 1999. "Value Addled." *Institutional Investor*, Vol. 33, No. 3 (March), pp. 58–68.

Banz, Rolf W. 1981. "The Relationship Between Market Value and Return of Common Stocks." *Journal of Financial Economics*, Vol. 9 (Nov.), pp. 3–18.

Beder, Tanya. 1995. "VaR: Seductive But Dangerous." *Financial Analysts Journal*, Sept. 10, pp. 12–24.

Bernstein, Peter. 1992. *Capital Ideas.* New York: The Free Press.

Bernstein, Peter. 1996. *Against the Gods: The Remarkable Story of Risk.* New York: John Wiley & Sons.

Bernstein, Peter. 1998. "Where, Oh Where Are the .400 Hitters of Yesteryear?" *Financial Analysts Journal*, Nov. 2, pp. 6–14.

Bernstein, Peter. 1999. "A New Look at the Efficient Market Hypothesis." *Journal of Portfolio Management*, Vol. 25 (Winter), p. 1.

Blin, John. 1997. "Risk for the Mathematically Disinclined." *Derivatives Strategy*, May, pp. 40–41.

Blin, John. 1999. "Arbitrage Pricing Theory." Applied Portfolio Technology, LTD website (www.aptltd.com).

Bogle, John C. 1998. *Investing with Simplicity.* Keynote speech, The Intelligent Investing Conference, The Philadelphia Inquirer, Philadelphia, PA, Oct. 3.

Bogle, John. 1998. "The First Index Mutual Fund: A History of Vanguard Index Trust and the Vanguard Index Strategy." The Vanguard Group website (www.vanguard.com).

Breit, William, and Roger W. Spencer (eds.). 1986. *Lives of the Laureates: Seven Nobel Economists*. Cambridge, MA: MIT Press.

Brown, Aaron. 1997. "The Next 10 VaR Disasters." *Derivatives Strategy*, March.

Brown, Ken. 1999. "The Reckoning." *Smart Money*, Feb., pp. 94–102.

Browning, E. S. 1997. "Where There's a Tax Cut, Wall Street Finds a Way." *Wall Street Journal*, Oct. 27, p. C1.

Butler, Jonathan. 1996. "Is Bigger Better—and for Whom?" *Worth*, Aug.

Burton, Jonathon. 1999. "Mispricing and Unrealistic Expectations." *Dow Jones Asset Management*, Mar. 4, pp. 21–28.

Carroll, Robert T. 1994–1999. "Occam's Razor." *Skeptic's Dictionary* website (www.skepdic.com).

Chancellor, Edward. 1999. *Devil Take the Hindmost: A History of Financial Speculation*. New York: Farrar Strauss Giroux.

Chow, George; Eric Jacquier; Mark Kritzman; and Kenneth Lowry. 1999. "Optimal Portfolios in Good Times and Bad." *Financial Analysts Journal*, May–June, pp. 65–73.

Clements, Jonathan. 1999. "How the Taxman Dines on Your Mutual Fund." *Wall Street Journal*, Aug. 31, p. C1.

Clow, Robert, and Riva Atlas. 1998. "What Went Wrong." *Institutional Investor* 32, No. 12 (Dec.), pp. 41–57.

Cohen, Tal. 1998. *Tal Cohen's Bookshelf* (www.forum2.org/tal/books).

Cooper, Christopher. 1999. "It's No Crude Joke: This Oil Field Grows Even as It's Tapped." *Wall Street Journal*, Nov. 12, p. A1.

Coy, Peter. 1997. "Mining Profits from Microdata." *Business Week*, Dec. 1.

Cronin, Isaac, and Raphael Pallais. 1985. *Champagne!* New York: Pocket Books.

Culp, Christopher; Ron Mensink; and Andrea Neves. 1999. "Value at Risk for Asset Managers." *Derivatives Weekly* (forthcoming).

Downing, Ned. 1999. "Revolutionary Idea." *Barron's*, Apr. 15, pp. 29–30.

Eco, Umberto. 1996. *The Island of the Day Before*. New York: Penguin.

Ehrbar, E. F. 1976. "Indexing: An Idea Whose Time Has Come." *Fortune*, June, pp. 142–147.

Ellis, Charles. 1985. *Investment Policy*. Chicago: Dow Jones Irwin.

Elton, Edwin J., and Martin J. Gruber. 1987. *Modern Portfolio Theory and Investment Analysis*. New York: John Wiley & Sons.

Fama, Eugene F. 1970. "Efficient Capital Markets: A Review of Theory and Empirical Work." *Journal of Finance*, Vol. 25, No. 2 (May), pp. 383–417.

Fama, Eugene F. 1998a. "Rethinking Stock Market Returns." *Capital Ideas*, January (University of Chicago Graduate School of Business Publications).

Fama, Eugene F. 1998b. "Value versus Growth: The International Evidence." *Journal of Finance*, Vol. 53, No. 6 (Dec.).

Fama, Eugene F., and Kenneth French. 1996. "Multifactor Explanations of Asset Pricing Anomalies." *Journal of Finance*, Vol. 51, pp. 55–84.

Fisher, Kenneth, and Meir Statman. 1999. "A Behavioral Framework for Time Diversification." *Financial Analysts Journal*, May 6, pp. 87–99.

Fritz, Michael. 1999. "Bond Index Funds Wield Better Yields." *Investment-News*, Nov. 5, p. 24.

Galbraith, John Kenneth. 1961. *The Great Crash of 1929*. Cambridge, MA: Riverside Press.

Gallacher, William R. 1994. *Winner Take All*. Chicago: Probus.

Gatev, Evan G.; William N. Goetzmann; and K. Geert Rouwenhorst. 1999. "Pairs Trading: Performance of a Relative Value Arbitrage Rule." Working paper, Yale School of Management.

Geisst, Charles R. 1997. *Wall Street: A History*. New York: Oxford University Press.

Gould, Carole. 1998. "Poof! For More and More Mutual Funds, a Quick Disappearing Act." *New York Times*, Aug. 16, p. 11.

Gray, Jack. 1997. "Overquantification." *Financial Analysts Journal*, Nov.–Dec., pp. 5–12.

Grossman, Sanford, and Joseph E. Stiglitz. 1980. "On the Impossibility of Informationally Efficient Markets." *American Economic Review*, June, pp. 393–408.

Haim, Larry, and Marshall Sarnat. 1984. *Portfolio and Investment Selection: Theory and Practice*. Englewood Cliffs, NJ: Prentice Hall.

Hansell, Saul. 1989. "Inside Morgan Stanley's Black Box." *Institutional Investor*, May, pp. 204–216.

Harrod, Ray. 1951. *The Life of John Maynard Keynes*. New York: W. W. Norton.

Harvey, John. 1996. "Heuristic Judgment Theory." The University of Colorado website (www.csf.colorado.edu).

Haugen, Robert. 1990. *Modern Investment Theory*. Englewood Cliffs, NJ: Prentice Hall.

Heritage Foundation. 1998. "The History of Taxation." The Heritage Foundation website (www.taxation.org).

Herman, Tom. 1999. "Tax Report." *Wall Street Journal*, Sept. 8, p. A1.

Hong, Harrison, and Jeremy C. Stein. 1998. "A Unified Theory of Underreaction, Momentum Trading, and Overreaction in Asset Markets." *Journal of Finance* (forthcoming).

Hong, Harrison; Terrence Lim; and Jeremy C. Stein. 1999. "Bad News Travels Slowly: Size, Analyst Coverage, and the Profitability of Momentum Strategies." *Journal of Finance* (forthcoming).

Horowitz, Donald L., and Robert J. Mackay. 1995. "Derivatives: State of the Debate," in Richard Teweles, Frank Jones, and Ben Warwick, eds. 1999. *The Futures Game*. Chicago: McGraw-Hill, 1999.

Institutional Investor Forum, 1999. "Mainstreaming Derivatives." *Institutional Investor*, Aug., p. 160.

Investor Home, 1999. The Investor Home website. (www.investorhome.com).

Jagadesh, Narashimhan, and Sheridan Titman. 1993. "Returns to Buying Winners and Selling Losers: Implications for Stock Market Efficiency." *Journal of Finance*, Vol. 48, pp. 65–91.

Jeffrey, Robert H., and Robert D. Arnott. 1993. "Is Your Alpha Big Enough to Cover Its Taxes?" *The Journal of Portfolio Management*, Spring, pp. 15–25.

Kahneman, Daniel, and Mark W. Riepe. 1998. "Aspects of Investor Psychology." *Journal of Portfolio Management*, Vol. 24, No. 4 (Summer).

Katona, George. 1975. *Psychological Economics*. New York: Elsevier Publishing Company.

Keynes, John M. 1936. *The General Theory of Employment, Interest, and Money*. New York: Harcourt, Brace & Company.

Khin, John. 1996. "To Load or Not to Load: A Study of the Marketing and Distribution Charges of Mutual Funds. *Financial Analysts Journal*, May 6, pp. 28–36.

Lawson, Tony, and Hashem Pesaran (eds.). 1985. *Keynesian Economics*. Armonk, NY: M. E. Sharpe.

LeBaron, Dean. 1998. *The Ins and Outs of Institutional Investing*. Dean LeBaron website (www.deanlebaron.com).

Lebon, Gustave, and Charles Mackay. 1994. *The Crowd and Extraordinary Popular Delusions*. Greenville, NC: Traders Press.

Lederman, Jess, and Robert A. Klein (eds.). 1996. *Market Neutral: State of the Art Strategies for Every Market Environment*. New York: McGraw-Hill.

Lewis, Michael. 1990. *Liar's Poker*. New York: Penguin Books.

Lewis, Michael. 1999. "How the Eggheads Cracked." *New York Times Magazine*, Jan. 24, pp. 24–42.

Lin, Po-Han. 1996. The Beethoven Depot website (www.edepot.com).

Lo, Andrew, and A. Craig MacKinley. 1999. *A Non-Random Walk Down Wall Street*. Princeton, NJ: Princeton University Press.

Loeb, Gerald M. 1996. *The Battle for Investment Survival*. New York: John Wiley & Sons.

Lux, Hal. 1998. "Extreme Finance." *Institutional Investor*, Oct., pp. 45–49.

Lux, Hal. 1998. "Hedge Fund? Who, Me?" *Institutional Investor*, Aug., pp. 33–36.

Lux, Hal, and Jack Willoughby. 1999. "May Day II." *Institutional Investor*, Jan., pp. 45–46.

Maital, Shlomo. 1982. *Minds, Markets, and Money*. New York: Basic Books.

Malkiel, Burton G. 1996. *A Random Walk Down Wall Street*. New York: W W Norton.

Markham, Jerry W. 1987. *The History of Commodity Futures Trading and Its Regulation*. New York: Praeger Publishing.

Marmer, Harry S. 1996. "Visions of the Future: The Distant Past, Yesterday, Today, and Tomorrow." *Financial Analysts Journal*, May–June, pp. 9–12.

McEnally, Richard, and Carl Ackerman. 1999. "The Returns of Hedge Funds: Risk, Return, and Incentives." *Journal of Finance* (forthcoming).

McGough, Robert, and Steve Liesman. 1999. "Wall Street Leaves Billions on the Table in Oil Mergers." *Wall Street Journal*, May 11, p. C1.

McIntyre, Robert. 1997. "Tax Shelters: The Video Game." *Slate*, Oct. 24.

McQueen, Grant, and Steve Thorley. 1999. "Mining Fool's Gold." *Financial Analysts Journal*, March–April 1999, pp. 61–71.

Miller, Jeffrey, and Peter J. Brennan. 1989. *Program Trading*. New York: J. K. Lasser.

New Bedford Whaling Museum. 1999. The History of Whaling website. (www.whalingmuseum.org).

Neyer, Ron. 1997. "Breaking Down NFC Superiority." *ESPN Sports Zone*, Jan. 17; ESPN website (www.espn.go.com).

nflhistory.com, 1998. "The History of Football." NFL website (www.nflhistory.com).

Niederhoffer, Roy. 1999. "Hedge Against What?" *Barron's*, Feb. 1.

Niederhoffer, Victor. 1997. *The Education of a Speculator*. New York: John Wiley & Sons.

Nobel Foundation, The. 1997. The Nobel Foundation website (www.nobel.se).

Odean, Terrance. 1998. "Are Investors Reluctant to Realize Their Losses?" Working paper, Graduate School of Management, University of California, Davis.

Odean, Terrance. 1999. "Do Investors Trade Too Much?" *American Economic Review* (forthcoming).

Perold, Andre F., and Robert S. Salomon, Jr. 1991. "The Right Amount of Assets Under Management." *Financial Analysts Journal*, May 6, pp. 31–39.

Picerno, James. 1998. "Bull Market Blues." *Dow Jones Asset Management*, May 6, pp. 32–38.

Picerno, James. 1999. "Alarming Efficiency." *Institutional Investor*, May 6, pp. 43–48.

Pitatelli-Palmarino, Massimo. 1994. *Inevitable Illusions: How Mistakes of Reason Rule Our Minds*. New York: John Wiley & Sons.

Putnam, Bluford. 1996. "Portable Alpha and Gearing Sharpe Ratios." *Global Investor*, Nov.

Putnam, Bluford. 1997a. "An Investment Paradigm for the New Millennium." *Global Investor*, Sept.

Putnam, Bluford. 1997b. "The High Cost of Investment Constraints." *Global Investor*, Nov.

Putnam, Bluford. 1998a. "What Is Market Neutral Anyway?" *Global Investor*, May.

Putnam, Bluford. 1998b. "Risk Management for Banks and Funds Is Not the Same Game." *Global Investor*, Sept.

Rekenthaler, John. 1999. "The Long Wait." *Dow Jones Asset Management*, Jan. 2, pp. 31–36.

Reltz, Michael. 1999. "Winner's Curse." *Worth Magazine*, Feb.

Roll, Richard, and Stephen A. Ross. 1984. "The Arbitrage Pricing Theory Approach to Strategic Portfolio Planning." *Financial Analysts Journal*, May–June, pp. 14–26.

Samuelson, Paul. 1974. "Challenge to Judgment." *Journal of Portfolio Management*, Fall.

Seward, Desmond. 1979. *Monks and Wine*. New York: Crown Publishing.

Sharpe, William F. 1962. "A Simplified Model for Portfolio Analysis." *Management Science*, Vol. 9, pp. 277–293.

Sharpe, William F. 1964. "Capital Asset Prices: A Theory of Market Equilibrium Under Conditions of Risk." *Journal of Finance*, Vol. 19, No. 3, pp. 425–442.

Sherden, William A. 1998. *The Fortune Sellers*. New York: John Wiley & Sons.

Shleifer, Andrei, and Robert W. Vishney. 1997. "The Limits of Arbitrage." *Journal of Finance*, Vol. 52, No. 1 (March), pp. 35–55.

Sobel, Robert. 1968. *Wall Street: America's Financial Disasters*. New York: MacMillan.

Sobel, Robert. 1999. "Mania Milestones." *Barron's*, Feb. 22.

Sullivan, Ryan; Allan Timmermann; and Halbert White. 1998. "Data Snooping, Technical Trading Rule Performance, and the Bootstrap." *Journal of Finance* (forthcoming).

Taubes, Gary. 1998. "Wall Street Smarts." *Discover*, Oct., pp. 105–112.

Taylor, Walton, and James Yoder. 1994. "Mutual Fund Trading Activity and Investor Utility." *Financial Analyst Journal*, May 6, pp. 66–69.

Teweles, Richard; Frank Jones; and Ben Warwick (eds.). 1999. *The Futures Game*. Chicago: McGraw-Hill.

Thomas, Gordon, and Max Morgan-Witts. 1908. *The Day the Bubble Burst*. New York: Doubleday & Co.

Tobin, James. 1958. "Liquidity Preference as Behavior Towards Risk." *Review of Economic Studies*, Vol. 67, pp. 65–86.

Treynor, Jack. 1999. "Zero Sum." *Financial Analysts Journal*, Jan.–Feb., pp. 8–12.

Tully, Shawn. 1998. "How the Smart Money Really Invests." *Money*, July 6.

United Press Syndicate. 1999. Calvin and Hobbes website (www.calvin andhobbes.com).

University of St. Andrews. 1997. The History of Mathematics website (www-history.mcs.st-andrews.ac.uk).

Vonnegut, Kurt. 1999. *Breakfast of Champions*. New York: Delta.

Warwick, Ben. 1996. *Event Trading*. Chicago: Irwin.

Wilford, D. Sykes, and Jose Mario Quintana. 1998. "The Unfettered Manager Is the Successful Manager." *Global Investor*, Oct.

Williams, John B. 1938. *The Theory of Investment Value*. Cambridge: Harvard University Press.

Yergin, Daniel. 1991. *The Prize*. New York: Simon and Schuster.

Zweig, Jason. 1999. "Confessions of a Fund Pro." *Money*, Feb., pp. 73–75.

Index